Angels Laughing

The Very Best Spiritual & Religious Humor

Compiled and written by Thomas Haka

Note for Librarians: A cataloguing record for this book is available from Library and Archives
Canada at www.collectionscanada.ca/amicus/index-e.html
ISBN 1-4120-5790-6

*Printed on paper with minimum 30% recycled fibre. Trafford's print shop
runs on "green energy" from solar, wind and other environmentally-friendly power sources.*

Offices in Canada, USA, Ireland and UK
This book was published *on-demand* in cooperation with Trafford Publishing. On-demand
publishing is a unique process and service of making a book available for retail sale to the
public taking advantage of on-demand manufacturing and Internet marketing. On-demand
publishing includes promotions, retail sales, manufacturing, order fulfilment, accounting and
collecting royalties on behalf of the author.

Book sales for North America and international:
Trafford Publishing, 6E–2333 Government St.,
Victoria, BC v8t 4p4 CANADA
phone 250 383 6864 (toll-free 1 888 232 4444)
fax 250 383 6804; email to orders@trafford.com
Book sales in Europe:
Trafford Publishing (uk) Limited, 9 Park End Street, 2nd Floor
Oxford, UK ox1 1hh UNITED KINGDOM
phone 44 (0)1865 722 113 (local rate 0845 230 9601)
facsimile 44 (0)1865 722 868; info.uk@trafford.com
Order online at:
trafford.com/05-0690

10 9 8 7 6 5 4

Table of Contents

Introduction

This book started with a good joke. This was a great joke I heard many years ago that I had trouble remembering the next day. I tried telling it anyway and ruined the punch line (know the feeling?). So, for the past twenty years I have been keeping joke notes to help me remember my favorites. This joke file has gotten pretty thick and with the advent of the Internet, it has been virtually bursting at the seams with the best jokes I've heard or received from friends.

Last year, I was sharing one of these jokes with some friends during a weekly spiritual discussion. Everyone laughed and so I continued to search my files for more spiritually-related humor to share each week.

After a few months I realized that it was getting more difficult to find jokes in my files that were genuinely funny and still suitable for spiritual seekers. I checked the library and several bookstores and was disappointed to find no <u>one</u> good book source for spiritual jokes.

The only books I found were joke books with a chapter or two on spiritual and religious subjects. But most of the material in them had been repeated so often that it was no longer funny. There were a few books on spiritual humor but these contained personal stories of such length that they made re-telling difficult.

It was at this point that I decided to put together a volume of the best anecdotes, jokes and puns that I could find, adapt or write myself. I wanted to keep them tied to a spiritual and religious theme (some loosely) and this immediately eliminated a lot of jokes on other subjects.

Another half of the remaining jokes no longer seemed funny to me and were thrown out. I started researching, adding and writing new jokes to expand the size of this volume. For ease of sharing, I picked a larger typeface that would be readable by most without glasses.

The first story I have included is one that made me laugh

over thirty years ago. There are many well-worn favorites that you may find missing from this volume - not because I didn't find them, but because they no longer appealed to me.

I have included some very old repeated jokes and particular puns that may seem tired to the reader but which still make me smile. This is the standard I felt I had to apply in deciding what to include - that which I still liked best.

My personal tastes will not be shared by all. I have made an effort to exclude the profane, obscene and overtly tasteless. But I still find there is a remaining undercurrent of irreverence and indelicacy that may bother some readers. I kept this material anyway because I have come to believe that taking ourselves and God too seriously can be boring and limiting to our growth as spiritual Beings.

This volume is in keeping with a spiritual ideal that is consistent with peace, love and joy. A God that lightens the heart in the midst of difficulties. A God that celebrates life in any and all of its myriad forms. A God of good humor that can be found in every religious tradition.

Humor, at it's best, breaks down many of the barriers that seem to separate us from each other. A shared laugh calls for no response and lets the heart open to join with others at a deeper level.

I hope that you find a laugh or more within this volume to enjoy and share. And if any story or expression bothers you too much, just rip it out!
The World is yours to create ---
 Just please pay for it first.

Laughter is the enemy of Fear.

Section One

Tales with a Twist

Finding Joy in Unexpected Places.

THE GOLDEN SCREW

A baby was born to a young minister and his wife. The child was a perfect little boy, handsome and well-formed. The only thing awry was that the baby had been born with a golden, grooved metal spot completely covering the boy's navel area.

The boy grew to manhood and everyone but the young man soon forgot about the golden navel. He consulted doctors and experts from around the world to find out the meaning of his strange golden anomaly. His seeking was to no avail as no one had ever seen anything quite like it.

In desperation, the young man turned to prayer. He received a vision directing him to seek a certain spiritual master who lived somewhere in Tibet. This wizened Guru was rumored to live alone sitting on the top of a high mountain peak.

Trusting his vision, the young man set out on this arduous journey to this remote mountain in the middle of winter. Climbing alone to the top of the snow-covered peak, he found the master meditating. As he approached, the ancient Guru's eyes opened in welcome. In a soft angelic voice the Guru spoke,

"I KNOW YOUR HEART YOUNG MAN & KNOW WHY YOU HAVE COME. I CANNOT EXPLAIN YOUR STRANGE AFFLICTION BUT I CAN TAKE IT FROM YOU IF YOU SO WISH."

The young man hesitated only for a second, before answering,

" YES, OH ANCIENT ONE. I WISH TO APPEAR AS EVERYONE ELSE. I AM TIRED OF THIS GOLDEN NAVEL AND ASK THAT IT BE TAKEN AWAY."

As the young man stood there, the old man nodded and raised his arms toward the sky.
A strange feeling tugged at the young man's innards and he opened his shirt to expose his stomach. Looking down, he saw the golden

spot on his navel quivering violently. Then, as he watched, the spot began to rotate counterclockwise.

A golden-threaded shaft gently eased itself outward. And, with a soft plunk, a golden screw fell out upon the frozen ground.

The young man observed that in it's place there was a perfect belly button (an in-ny), which the screw had formerly hidden. In ecstatic joy the young man leaped with enthusiasm. Then, as he bent down to thank the Great Guru.... his BUTT FELL OFF!

THE DUCKS

Three single women, who happened to be close friends, died together in an auto accident while they were on their way to church. A lovely Angel whisked them from their bodies and escorted them to the gates of Heaven. Waiting for them was Saint Peter.

"Welcome to Heaven," he said, as the Pearly Gates opened wide before them. Stepping inside, they gazed in wonder at the infinite beauty that surrounded them. The only puzzlement was the thousands of ducks that wandered everywhere. Saint Peter explained that the many ducks were much loved by God himself, and that the only rule in Heaven was,

"Don't step on the ducks."

The three friends waved good-bye to Saint Peter and set off to explore the many raptures of their new home. The trees seemed lit in a fury of fall colors all of the time, beautiful waterfalls flowed endlessly into dazzling gardens and loving people smiled on them as they passed.

Then, the first friend must have gotten lost looking up at the Auroras in the sky and she stepped on a small duck. A loud thunder shook Heaven and Saint Peter reappeared with the ugliest man they had ever seen. Saint Peter took the wrist of the first friend and with a rough metal shackle, attached her to the arm of the ugly gnome-like man.

"Your punishment for stepping on one of God's ducks is to spend eternity chained to this afflicted man."

The two remaining friends looked on in horror as the ugly creature hauled their friend into a cave in the nearby hill. Saint Peter again disappeared, leaving the two women with their thoughts.

Sadness for their friend must have interfered with their awareness though - as after barely ten more steps, the second friend also stepped on a duck!

With another crack of thunder Saint Peter was back. This time he had an even more hideous man with him who drooled lasciviously as he was manacled to the wrist of the second woman. The last woman watched as the loathsome creature disappeared dragging her friend behind him.

Quite shaken by these experiences, the last woman removed herself to a part of Heaven where there were no ducks to step upon. It was still beautiful but it didn't have the lovely lake where the ducks seemed to live.

Several months went by without incident. For, even in this part of Heaven, the woman was careful before taking any steps. Heaven was beautiful and the people friendly but the woman was feeling a little lonely and missed her two friends.

Saint Peter seemed to be sensing her need for companionship as he appeared before her the next day. With Saint Peter was the most handsome man the woman had ever seen. He was tall, muscular, with beautiful eyes and a soft smile. Taking the woman's hand, Saint Peter ceremoniously placed it in the hand of the attractive stranger and bound the two wrists together with a golden cord.

As Saint Peter left them the woman looked into her new partner's eyes shyly and gratefully said aloud, "I am so grateful for your company. I'm not sure what I have done to deserve such a wonderful companion."

To this the attractive stranger replied, "I don't know about you lady, but I stepped on a duck!"

THE BELL RINGER

In a small French country town a magnificent cathedral had been built many hundreds of years ago. The church attracted worshipers from around the world and it was known far and wide for the lovely tones of its church bells.

One day the church's bishop was notified that the old man who rang the bells had died in his sleep.

Later that week the bishop started wondering what he should do about replacing the bell ringer. So, the next day he posted an announcement on the church bulletin board advertising that the position as bell ringer was now open.

Days passed and no one stepped forward to apply for the position. The worried bishop realized that a major holiday was soon coming and the church bells were still silent.

More days passed before the bishop woke to the sound of a pounding on his front door. Wiping the sleep from his eyes, he opened the door to find a large man with no arms standing in front of him. The armless man stated his desire to become the new bell ringer for the church.

The bishop asked the man how he expected to perform these duties without any arms. The man confidently replied,

"Watch this."

With that, the man climbed to the top of the bell tower with the curious bishop trailing behind. At the top, the man took a running start and threw himself at the nearest of the two bells. His head struck it a glancing blow and the huge bell chimed perfectly in response. The amazed bishop asked if this wasn't terribly painful to the man?

"No, I was born with a very strong endurance to pain and it is only rapture I feel."

The armless man then threw himself at the second bell. But this time he misjudged the distance, slipped and fell screaming to the street far below.

The horrified bishop raced down the tower stairs to find the armless man lying lifeless on the ground surrounded by curious on-lookers. The crowd asked,
"Who was he?"

To this the bishop could only answer,
"I don't know. But his face rings a bell."

****

A week after the unfortunate incident, the bishop woke to the sound of a pounding at his door. Standing before him was an armless man struggling to force his way in.

"What do you want?" asked the bishop.

The man answered that he was the dead bell ringer's twin brother. He had come to replace his brother and show that arms were not necessary to ring the bells properly.

Before the bishop could reply, the man dashed up the stairs to the bell tower. At the top, the armless man raced toward the nearest bell headfirst.

The bishop was unable to warn him that the bell had been immobilized for repairs. The armless man smashed into the stationary bell and with a look of astonishment still on his face, fell to his death on the street below.

Again, there was a gathering of townspeople around the body. Again, they looked to the bishop for an answer. This time all he could say about the deceased stranger was,

"He was a dead ringer for the other one."

WISHES

A young minister had just married the beautiful leader of his church choir. They were honeymooning at a nearby lake resort and the minister was showing his new bride how to skip rocks across the placid lake's surface.

The young woman had much musical talent but had not had the opportunity to play sports or develop her physical coordination outside of the recital halls. But, determined to please her new husband, she took the flat rock he handed to her and unleashed it with all her strength toward the nearby water.

Regrettably, there was an expensive vacation home located next door and her energetic throw took an errant turn and the stone smashed loudly through its large picture window.

Aghast, the minister tried to comfort his now-sobbing wife. He explained that they would go up to the house together and explain exactly what had happened, that it was an accident, and that they would make amends together.

So, the two of them went to the neighbor's house and knocked at the large impressive front door.

A deep but friendly voice answered,
"Please come in."

The couple entered the house and was appalled at the damage visible around them. Not only was the huge picture window shattered, but also the stone had continued into the house destroying a mirror and smashing a beautiful old antique bottle resting on a table nearby.

A rotund white-bearded man sat amongst the destruction peacefully looking at the frightened couple and he asked,
"Are you the ones responsible for this?'

The young minister stepped forward and replied,
"Yes. But it was an accident and we wish to pay for any repairs."
(Yet at the same time he was mentally adding up the extent of the costly damage and fingering his thin wallet.)

The minister was surprised then as the portly, bearded gent rose from his seat and welcomed him with a warm handshake and the words,

"No apology is necessary. It is I who must thank you! You see I am a powerful genie who has been trapped in that bottle for over two hundred years. You have set me free and as a reward I am allowed to grant three wishes. I will grant you each one of the wishes, but if you don't mind, I will keep one for myself."

The relieved minister looked at the benevolent genie and thought hard for a moment before asking,

"Can you grant me a million dollars every year so that I can do good works for the community and our church?"

The genie smiled and said,

"It is done. The money is already on it's way. And I will also see to it that you have a long and healthy life from which to do your good works."

Then, looking at the wife he asked,

"And what does your heart desire young woman?"

The minister's pretty blonde wife answered that she had always had this dream about having beautiful vacation homes in countries around the world where they could stay with their church friends and conduct retreats.

The genie answered, "As you speak the words, it is done. The titles for these luxury homes are being drawn up at this very moment. And I will see to it that they remain safe places for you and your friends."

The grateful young couple hugged themselves in gratitude for their remarkably good fortune. Then they remembered their new genie friend.... and together, they asked,

"And what is it that you will use your wish for?"

The genie now seemed a little shy and sad as he replied,

"I am not allowed to grant my own wish, but only to ask it aloud. I have been alone in my bottle for a very long time. My wish is for the company of a beautiful young woman just for one evening. And I would ask that your wife be the one to do me this great honor?"

The young minister looked at his wife and she looked back at him. The genie had done so much for them and he seemed like a gentle trustworthy type.

The wife nodded her head and the minister replied for both of them.

"I love my wife and I know she loves me. We are very grateful to you genie. And if her company will bring you happiness, I give my permission for her to spend the evening with you."

His wife also nodded her assent and the minister placed his wife's hand into the hand of the now-glowing genie. With a kiss to his wife's cheek, he backed out the door and told her he would see her soon.

Alone with the genie, the young wife now felt a bit unprepared. What would this genie want from her in their time together? A glint now shown in the genie's eyes as he looked carefully as his younger companion.

Her mouth dropped open in shock as the genie started removing his robe - and then he moved closer! She tried to pull away but the genie was very strong and pulled her to him. Their struggle ended on a nearby couch where the genie made love to the minister's wife. This lovemaking continued on and on. The genie seemed insatiable.

Finally, after four hours together, the genie took a break and looked into the exhausted wife's eyes and asked her how old she and her husband were,

"We're thirty-five," she responded breathlessly.

"Really?" he answered, "-and you still believe in genies?"

ADOPTION

The senior minister at a large prosperous midwestern church was approached by his wife while he was preparing his Sunday sermon. Stifling back her tears, she explained that their housekeeper had just given her notice and would be leaving at the end of the week.

This shouldn't have been a big deal, but this particular housekeeper was the best they had ever had, was hard-working and the woman had become close friends with many of the members of the congregation including the minister's wife.

The concerned minister asked why 'Helga' was leaving with such short notice. The minister's wife explained that she had already asked Helga the same question. Helga had sadly related the story of having met and fallen in love with a racecar driver. The man was now gone but Helga was with child.

The minister and his wife prayed together about what should be done. The next day they called Helga into the living room and announced that Helga should continue to live with them and the minister and his wife would adopt the baby girl.

Helga stayed with the minister, his wife and the new baby girl but, the following year, the minister's wife again consulted her husband.
"Helga has decided to leave again. She has met some traveling basketball player, fallen in love and is with child again."

A bit more upset this time at the woman's easy virtues, but not wanting to have to raise the one-year-old baby alone, the minister called Helga in and told her they would adopt this child as well.

A lovely baby boy was born and joined the little girl as part of the family. All seemed well until the following year when the minister's distraught wife entered his study crying.
"Don't tell me," roared the minister. "Has Helga met a football player this time?"

"No." whimpered his wife, "she just left me a note that

she has resigned."

"What!' exclaimed the minister, "After everything we have done for her. What was her reason?"

"She said she was leaving... because ... because, she hadn't signed on to work for such a large family."

NEAR DEATH EXPERIENCE

A young female minister named Mabel had a massive heart attack in the middle of her Sunday sermon and was rushed to the nearest hospital. She received an immediate operation but she remained in a coma for eight days before regaining consciousness.

While in the coma she had a near death-experience and while moving through a tunnel of white light, met a radiant being that she knew was Jesus Christ. Jesus had told her that her mission on Earth was not complete and that she must return but that they would meet again in forty years.

The minister cried as she related this story to the doctor at her bedside and wondered aloud what things she would need to do with her remaining forty years. The doctor assured her that her heart now appeared completely healed. He then suggested that while she was in the hospital she have a nose job, liposuction and a complete makeover so that she would look good no matter what it was she was supposed to do.

The minister agreed and ten days later looked into a mirror at her new thin self. Her hair was now two shades lighter and beautifully coifed. Her new slim nose matched her now thinner body. She felt ready to go out and do God's work.

She chatted happily to the cab driver as he drove her back to her home near the church. But as she got out of the cab and crossed the street, a teenager in a truck slammed into her and she was instantly killed.

She found herself back in the tunnel of white light. Ahead of her she saw Jesus. Upon reaching His side, she looked into His radiant eyes and inquired why He had not rescued her from the truck?

Jesus looked back at her closely.

"Mabel, Is that you? That's too bad ... I didn't recognize you."

THE FIRST MAN

Eve was alone in the Garden of Eden but was not happy. God came to her and asked what was wrong.

"God, this is a beautiful place you have created for me and I enjoy all the other creatures but I am still lonely for someone to talk to when you are not here."

"Well Eve, I think I have a solution. I will create a 'man' to keep you company. 'Man' is an aggressive, flawed creature with a huge ego. He'll be bigger and stronger and, though he will listen to you, he will not understand much. He will give you someone to talk to but are you willing to put up with all of his problems?"

"Oh yes God! When can you create him?"

"Well, I can probably do it tomorrow, but there is one other condition."

"What's that God?"

"You'll have to let him believe I created him first."

KILKENNEY

An Irish priest is headed down the street after imbibing a little too much of the communion wine. He bumps into a man in front of the church and asks him where he is from.

The man replies, "Kilkenney".

"Kilkenney? I can't believe it. I'm from Kilkenney too!
Won't you join me inside and we'll have a wee toast to Kilkenney."

The man agrees and together they toast Kilkenney. The priest then asks the man where he went to school.

The man answers "St. Joseph's".

"By God and Bygorrah! That's where I went to school. Let's have a drink to St. Joseph's."

"And where did you live in Kilkenney?"

The man relied "Haden Street."

"My God. The same street I meself called home for many years! Another toast to Haden Street."

Just then, two nuns walked into the rectory and one asked the other what was going on?

"Nothing much," said the older nun. "It's just the O'Brewski twins drinking again."

An Italian priest, A German Lutheran minister and a Chinese Zen master arrive in Heaven at the same time. God appears and tells the three that they may enter the gates of Heaven as soon as they can work together and move a huge pile of trash away from the gate.

After God leaves, the Italian priest volunteers to be in charge of shoveling, The German minister offers to do any sweeping up after the pile is moved and together they tell the Chinaman that all he has to do is take care of the supplies.

God returns the next day and is very angry. The pile of trash is still sitting in front of Heaven's gate. Avoiding God's angry gaze, the Italian priest stutters an apology.

"I so sorry. I no hav-a-no shovel. The Chinese fella was supposed to be in charge of the supplies and he has -as-a - disappeared. I could no find-a-him nowhere."

The Lutheran minister agreed.

"Ach! Dat Chinese fellow, He no get me zat broom iter."

God is really ticked off now and storms around the trash pile looking for the Chinese Zen master.

Just as he turns the corner, a pile of trash erupts in front of him and the Chinese guy pops out yelling,

"Supplies!"

VAMPIRES

Two Catholic Nuns, Grace and Prudence, are traveling together in Eastern Europe. One night they find themselves in front of a huge dilapidated castle in a remote section of Romania. It starts to rain and the sisters seek shelter in the old castle.

It gets darker and they find some candles inside and light them. Through the sound of the rain outside they hear a strange whirring of wings. In the candlelight, the terrified nuns watch as a hideous creature materializes near them. The creature is man - like but has a deformed face with leathery black wings attached to his body and huge protruding fangs in his mouth.

Screaming loudly, the two sisters dashed to the nearest door and pulled it closed behind them. It was in the nick of time, as the hideous creature threw himself at the door. Narrow iron bars in the door's window allowed them to see the creature as it tore at the barrier with its claws.

One of the nuns took out a bottle of holy water that she had picked up at the Vatican and opening it, splashed it between the bars onto the vampire's face.

The vampire screamed as the holy water burned his skin. But the creature keep hissing and pulling savagely at the door.

"What now, Sister Grace? What can we do?"

"Show him your cross, Sister Prudence. Maybe that will work."

"Are you sure?"

"Please Sister Prudence! Show him your cross. I can't think of anything else."

With that, Sister Prudence took a deep breath, opened the door and yelled loudly at the creature,

"Now you've got me angry! Get the hell out of here!"

PARALYSIS

A well-known and revered Catholic Archbishop was visiting Boston for the first time. A large formal dinner was arranged in his honor. He found himself seated that night next to a very attractive widow with whom he struck up a lively conversation.

Their talk wandered from spirituality, to economics and then to health issues. The Archbishop confided to the woman that he had remained healthy his entire life but still was consumed by irrational fears that he might someday become totally paralyzed.

The widow asked why he would think such an odd thing. Had he been paralyzed as a child?

"No." said the Archbishop, "But I have a family history of age-onset paralysis. First my father, then my mother and just last year my poor older brother."

"How sad," replied the widow? "Perhaps..."

Before she could finish her statement, the Archbishop jerked rigidly erect and proclaimed through clenched teeth.

"My God! It's happening.... I have total loss of feeling in my right leg."

The widow tried to calm the poor man down and whispered in his ear.

"It's all right Archbishop. I just want you to know that it is MY thigh that you have been pinching."

MATERIALISM

A very wealthy member of the congregation was parking his new BMW convertible on the street in front of the church. As he got out of the car, a speeding truck came by passing too close to the curb and it completely ripped the open door of the BMW from it's hinges.

The church's minister saw the truck speeding off and rushed over to help. He arrived to witness the owner screaming profanities at the truck driver and cursing the fact that his new BMW would never be the same again.

The minister was shocked by the man's language and attitude. Shaking his head in disgust, the minister upbraided the wealthy man by saying,

"Are you so lost in your materialistic views that you have forgotten where you are and the things that are most important?"

The wealthy man was still red in the face with anger and in his fury shouted back at the minister.

"How can you say such a thing? Didn't you see what happened? That *&%&$* !"

The minister responded with concern,

"My God man. Don't you even realize that your left arm is missing? It was ripped off in the accident and you're bleeding! Who cares about the condition of the car or the truck driver?"

The car owner looks down for the first time and notices his missing limb and with unabated fury shouts up to Heaven.

"Damn it all.... Not my new Rolex too!"

DINNER ALONE

A young rabbi was having dinner by himself at a new kosher restaurant that had just opened near the synagogue. He couldn't fail to notice as a gorgeous blond woman was seated at the table directly across from him. The blond lady smiles at him and places her napkin demurely in her lap.

The young rabbi is slightly embarrassed and looks away. Then he hears a loud sneeze and looks up to see the blond woman holding her nose. Gently rolling across the floor toward him is a glass eye.

The rabbi reaches down and retrieves the glass orb and returns it to the blond woman. The woman pops the eye back into its socket and thanks the young rabbi saying,

"Thank you so much. I'm so sorry.... Please, let me buy you your meal for your kindness."

The rabbi agrees and joins the young woman at her table. They have a wonderful meal together and enthusiastically talk about their lives and shared spiritual values.

After paying for everything, the blond invites the rabbi to her home for lunch the next day so that they can continue their conversation. The rabbi hesitates for a second, but then agrees to meet her.

Arriving at the blond woman's home the next day, the rabbi admires the cozy haven she has created for herself. It's a small older house with beautiful flowers in front and a garden in back. A nice fire is in the fireplace and there are fresh-cut flowers on the table.

He sits down to a gourmet meal that the woman has prepared by herself and they continue their conversation as they eat. Everything seems so perfect.

After dessert, the rabbi looks at the blond and says with obvious interest,

"You know, you really are the perfect woman. Very attractive, intelligent, a wonderful homemaker and cook. How is it that you have never married? Are you this nice to everyone you meet?"

"Oh no," she replies with a coy smile,
"You just happened to catch my eye."

RAFFLE PRIZES

Three Lutheran ministers in Northern Sweden got together to plan a joint winter festival for their three congregations. They decided that a church raffle would be a good way to raise the funds to pay for the festival. The big question was, what type of prize should they offer in the drawing?

Father Olaf shared that last year his church had offered free tickets to a Christmas play. The winning couple had seemed pleased but the playhouse had burned down during the summer.

Father Sven shared that his congregation had offered free lodging at the town's only hotel. But, until they offered indoor plumbing and got rid of the outhouse, something else might be better as a prize.

Father Lute just shook his head when it was his turn to share.

"Vell, I don't know dat I can 'elp. Lest yere, Ole's 'ardvare store donated dese toilet brushes. Vell, Inger an 'er sisters von dem at de raffle lest yere. She tol me de vas very nice, but now she tinks de vill be goin back to usin de toilet paper."

DATING A MINISTER

Two single women ministers were meeting for lunch. The first was a blonde named Rev. Mary who asked her brunette friend Rev. Rachel about a young man who happened to attend church in both their congregations.

"Rachel, I understand that you went out with Sam Mauler last month. He has asked me out too, and I wanted to talk to you first, before I give him an answer."

"Well Mary, He did show up for our date on time. He is a handsome man and he was impeccably dressed. He brought me a beautiful bouquet of flowers and held the door of his new convertible open for me. We went to dinner at an expensive restaurant, had a fabulous meal and then saw a great play afterwards.
He's a wonderful conversationalist with a witty sense of humor. I'd never had so much fun on a date. But, when we got back to my house, he tried to kiss me good night on my porch. When I resisted, he turned into an animal and began pawing at me and ripped my new dress. I finally had to push him away and slam the door."

"My Goodness Rachel, what a story. I guess I'm going to have to turn down that date."

"No Mary, don't do that. I'm just suggesting that maybe you shouldn't wear a new dress."

THE MOTHER-IN-LAW

A young rabbi and his wife had recently moved from New York City and were now living in Jerusalem. The wife's mother came to visit them in their new little house.

She complained constantly that Jerusalem was too hot, the house was too small and that the young rabbi was away too much. The young wife cried a lot and the young rabbi bit his lip and tried to endure the abuse.

The mother-in-law seemed happy to stay with them despite all her complaints. It was during the second week of her stay, that the mother-in-law went shopping by herself at the local street market.

While she was there, An Arab camel dealer lost control of one of his largest beasts and the wayward camel dashed away through the crowded bazaar. The camel was finally cornered next to where the mother-in-law was standing. In a last act of rebellion, the camel reared back and kicked into the crowd knocking the mother-in-law flat on her face.

The mother-in-law was taken to the nearest hospital, but despite efforts to revive the woman, she never recovered consciousness.

The young rabbi and his wife said prayers for their departed family member. After the final prayer, the local mortician arrived and asked to speak to the young rabbi.

The undertaker explained that the mother-in-law's body could be shipped back to New York for a price of $10,000. Or, she could be buried locally for only $500.. He knew the young rabbi was not rich and that the mother-in-law had few living relatives back in the United States. Did the young rabbi wish to find her a nice spot in the local cemetery?

No, insisted the young rabbi, they would find the money somehow and ship the body back to the U.S..

The undertaker was puzzled by this seeming extravagance and asked the rabbi if there was some special reason the woman's body should be shipped all the way back to New York?

The young rabbi took him aside and whispered,

"A man was buried here a few thousand years ago and rose from the dead.... I just can't take that chance!"

THE FLY

A disciple of the ancient sage Confucius was having dinner with a group of Buddhists. The food was delicious and the mood amenable until a large black fly began buzzing loudly as it circled the table.

At first the group did their best to ignore the fly, but this seemed to make it bolder as it landed on several food items and then buzzed into the Confucian guest's hair.

Bowing to the group, the Confucian reached for a nearby newspaper and proceeded to roll it into a formidable baton. In horror the Buddhists watched as the Confucian swung wildly at the intruding fly - doing his best to destroy the offending insect.

The Buddhists immediately began to meditate and pray for the souls of both the fly and their Confucian friend. The buzzing stopped and one of the Buddhists looked up. The fly was standing stationary in the middle of the table with its wings still vibrating.

Above the fly, the Confucian had the wadded up paper baton leveled and seemed ready to deliver a deathblow to the fly. But as the Buddhists watched, the Confucian looked deeply into the soul of the fly and put down his baton.

As the fly buzzed away, the group let out a collective sigh of relief for their guest's karmic reprieve. The mood of the group lightened again and his neighbor asked the Confucian what had gone through his mind at that last second with the fly.

The Confucian scratched his head, thought deeply, and replied that he was about to kill the fly, but that as he looked at

it very closely...
He realized it was the WRONG fly...

ELVIS

Father O'Grimy had spent twenty years serving a rural church. Now, after all that time, his parish had chipped in and was sending him to Las Vegas for a well-deserved vacation. He had never taken time for a vacation before, nor had he had time to leave the small town where he grew up and went to seminary school.

His plane ride to Las Vegas went flawlessly and he was reading the in-flight magazine. There was so much to see and so little time. His pleasant reverie was interrupted as the flight attendant came by, looked at the priest and shouted,

" Oh my God! It's Elvis... You're not dead after all."

Father O'Grimy looked around behind him and then to the sides. Then it dawned on him that the woman thought 'he' was Elvis. He looked the young attendant straight in the eyes and admonished,

"Don't be a fool young lady. I can assure you I am not Elvis."

After this strange encounter, Father O'Grimy made sure he was the first to de-plane and rushed to the baggage area. He got his suitcase and was the first to reach the taxi stand outside.

But, as the cab driver came around the vehicle to put his luggage in the trunk, the driver hesitated, looked at the priest and said,

"Oh my gosh... Elvis. I knew you weren't dead. I've always been one of you biggest fans."

Father O'Grimy was getting a little ticked-off by all this crazy talk and he wasted no time in telling the driver to,

"Stop all this foolishness. I'm not Elvis or anything like him. Now take me to my hotel."

Father O'Grimy barely had time to stop fuming in the back of the cab before they arrived at the beautiful resort where he would be staying. Ignoring the still-staring cab driver, he got his own bag and entered the hotel lobby.

But, at the hotel desk he had not yet received his room key when the hotel manager came up to him and loudly exclaimed,

"ELVIS! We knew the stories weren't true. We knew you'd be back some day. We kept your old suite ready for you - the one with the Jacuzzi; built in bar, loaded buffet table and an up - dated list of young show girl's numbers. Welcome back."

To which, Father O'Grimy scrunched up his face and replied,

"Well thank you...Thank you very muchhh."

THE WAVE

An old Jewish rabbi took his only grandson to see the Pacific Ocean. They were walking along the rugged coast together when an enormous wave washed ashore and inundated the pair.

The old rabbi grabbed desperately at a nearby rock as the wave threatened to tear him free and pull him under. Completely soaked, but managing to hold onto the rock, the rabbi watched as the huge wave pulled his grandson out into the ocean depths.

The boy screamed once and then disappeared into the distance. The old rabbi reached out in despair but realized his grandson was gone. Bemoaning his fate, but looking up to Heaven, the rabbi prayed with a fervent intensity,

"Oh God! Why! Why! Why, take my only grandson? My son and daughter-in-law entrusted him to my care and they will never understand what has happened. I have served you devotedly my entire life. Please! Please God.... Return my grandson to me."

The sky darkened and seemed to rumble in response. Another huge wave crashed towards the beach. The rabbi got back out of it's way and watched as the crest of the wave broke near his feet and deposited the wet, but still-breathing body of his young grandson.

Looking up again to the heavens, the old rabbi spoke once more to God.

"He had a hat on too..."

NATIONAL PARK

An Islamic mullah and a Czechoslovakian priest were at an inter-denominational conference together in Alaska. Despite the differences in their faiths, the two men had become friendly and decided to visit one of the nearby national parks together at the end of the conference.

At the park entrance they were warned that it was the mating season for the park bears and that they could become dangerous. But, despite the warning, the two men decided to continue their visit, having promised the ranger that they would report in every day.

The next day there was no news from the two men and two of the park rangers decided to go out and investigate what had happened.

The rangers managed to find the mullah and priest's campsite but were wary because the men's tent was severely damaged and there were large bear prints all around the area. Picking out the freshest set of bear tracks, they followed them out into the woods.

From the tracks, there seemed to be at least two bears traveling together.... probably a male and female. It took the rangers several hours to finally track the bears to their den. Outside the den a large female bear was lounging on a rock with her muzzle covered in blood.

Fearing the worse, the rangers shot the female bear with their tranquilizer gun and when the bear dropped into a stupor, they investigated more closely. Sure enough, inside the bear's mouth were the remnants of the mullah's robe.

Horrified, the two rangers looked at each other. Then one of the rangers started to utter the obvious truth.....

"You know what this means..."

"Yes," said the other one, "the Czech is in the male."

DEMOCRACY

Four Israeli rabbis had recently immigrated to the United States. After arriving in New York, the men decided to meet together each week to read the Torah and discuss theology. One of these 'discussions' led to a disagreement between the men and the oldest rabbi had decreed that, to keep the peace, they would try in the future, to be more democratic. They would abide by the majority's opinion in each scriptural interpretation.

This sounded fair, but it upset the youngest of the four rabbis. Though the youngest, he had attended university and felt that intellectually, he was much more capable than the older men who seemed 'locked' into the old ways. Almost every 'discussion' ended with him disagreeing with the other rabbis and being voted down three to one.

The youngest rabbi tried to swallow his pride but it finally reached a boiling point one day when the other rabbis kept insisting that there was no possibility that Jesus' teachings had any value. Again, he was voted down three to one when he tried to persuade them to keep an open mind on the subject.

In desperation, the young rabbi cast his arms skyward and appealed to God directly,

"Oh, God. Please hear my heart as I ask you to send us a sign that you are listening and that there is some truth in my words about Jesus."

The beautiful sunny day turned dark as black clouds obscured the sky.

"Look, Look." cried the young rabbi, "God is giving us a sign that I am correct."

The other rabbis disagreed and pointed out that clouds often form on warm summer days and this was just an act of nature, not God.

"Please God, give us a greater sign that they may know."

The sky got darker and lightening bolts flashed around them hitting and destroying the nearest tree. But the older rabbis were not impressed and insisted it was just part of an ordinary storm.

The young rabbi started to call forth once more for a sign that they would not fail to recognize, but his plea was interrupted by a deep voice coming from the sky itself.

"He is right! This is the word of your Lord and God."

The clouds began to dissipate as the four rabbis looked skyward in rapt amazement. Then the oldest rabbi cleared his throat and announced,

"Well, I guess that makes it three to two..."

LOTTERY WINNER

The grumpy old minister's young wife arrived at her home unexpectedly in the middle of the day, dashed into the house, ran up the stairs to the parson's study and shouted at the top of her lungs,
"Jackson, pack your bags. I won the damn state lottery!"

The Reverend Jackson replies,
"That's wonderful Edith! But please don't use profanity. Anyway, what should I pack? My beach stuff or some of my mountain stuff?"
She replies,
"Don't matter. Just get the hell out!"

TICK - TOCK

A Baptist minister was visiting Germany and staying at his parent's ancestral home. The old home was still in good shape but the minister noticed that the only clock in the house was a huge grandfather's clock and that it kept stopping in the middle of the night and going 'tick, tic, tick' instead of 'tick tock'.

Even though the old clock was very heavy, the minister managed to get it into a wheelbarrow and took it into the nearby town to get it repaired. The village clockmaker's shop door was open and a large man with a 'Hitler' mustache was sitting at the counter. The man looked up menacingly as the Baptist minister approached, and asked in a heavy Teutonic accent,

"Vat sims to be ze problem?"

"I don't know. This clock seems to stop each night no matter how much I wind it …. and it goes 'tick, tick' instead of 'tick, tock'."

The huge man then opens up the back of the clock and spends the next hour wrestling with the clock's innards. He then puts it back together, sets the hour hand and together they listen to the clock go, 'Tick, Tick, Tick'.

Cursing under his breath, the shopkeeper with the big mustache goes into a nearby cupboard and pulls out an enormous flashlight and a humongous screwdriver. He clicks the flashlight on and waving it in front of the clock he says in a threatening tone,

"Ve haf vays of making you tock!"

THE HANGING

A preacher drives into an old western town. It seemed to be deserted and all but one of the shops is empty. Going into the one open shop, the preacher asks the storekeeper where everyone has gone. The grizzled old storekeeper explains,

"They've gone to the hanging."

"Hanging?" says the minister, "who are they hanging?"

"Newspaper Bob".

"Newspaper Bob?" repeats the minister. "That's a strange name. Does he run a newspaper?"

"Naw! He just wears them. A newspaper hat, a newspaper shirt, newspaper pants, newspaper coat, newspaper shoes...."

That's really strange, thought the minister before asking,

"What are they hanging him for?"

"Rustling."

A Hasidic rabbi was walking through the streets of New York City. As he paused at a stoplight, a young well-built man in a sweatshirt next to him asked what time it was.

The rabbi seemingly ignored the young man's question even though the rabbi's watch was visible on his wrist.

"Excuse me," said the young man, "could you give me the time?"

The rabbi continued to ignore the young man's one simple question and proceeded across the intersection when the light changed. The young man continued across the intersection as well, and cornered the rabbi at the next stoplight.

"Sir. Please tell me why you won't just look at your watch and give me the time?"

"Well," the rabbi started, "I don't know you. You look like a stranger to the city. If I tell you the time, I might feel obligated to help you out and even take you home with me. At home I have two pretty, unmarried daughters. You are young and handsome. You'll probably fall in love with one of them and then want to get married. Tell me ... what would I need with a son-in-law who can't even afford a watch?"

A HELPFUL PRAYER

A woman was struck by a speeding cab as she tried to cross a busy street in Boston. The cab driver rushed to her side and a crowd of on-lockers gathered around the broken, bleeding body. One tried to stop the bleeding but the woman was already very far gone.

"Someone get a priest!"

But there were no priests, no ministers and no rabbis in the vicinity. Finally, an older man stepped out from the crowd and announced that, though he wasn't an ordained clergyman, he had lived next door to Saint Margaret's Church his entire life. He said he had overheard quite a bit of the Catholic liturgy over those years and perhaps he could remember enough of it now, to provide some comfort to the dying woman.

The crowd parted to let the little man through. Kneeling by the woman's side he took her hand in his own, blessed it with the sign of the cross, and recited over her,
" B-10, I-17,N-30, G-47......."

SUTRA

A learned Buddhist monk was making a long trek through the mountains of Tibet. He carried with him some of the collected sayings of the Buddha, known as the 'Sutra'. His deep knowledge and understanding of the 'Sutra' were widely respected and the monk often used to read from and explain the 'Sutra' to lay - people to deepen their spiritual awareness.

He also did this to provide some return for the generosity that was universally extended to him.

One day as the monk reached the edge of a great river, he came upon an old woman selling tea and cakes at the side of the path. The tired and hungry monk spoke to the old woman and offered to give her the benefits of his great learning from the 'Sutra' in return for some tea and cakes.

The old woman seemed unimpressed with his offer and countered with one of her own.

"Wandering monk, answer me one question using your great book and I will give you the tea and cookies you have requested."

The monk readily agreed and waited for her question.

"When you are eating these cakes, are you eating them with the mind of the past, the mind of the present or the mind of the future."

The monk was puzzled by this question and taking out his copy of the 'Sutra' poured over its contents looking for the right answer. Daylight soon faded and the old woman packed up her things to leave. But before she left she shook her head and said to the speechless monk,

"Foolish monk! You eat the cakes with your mouth."

GOTTCHA

A priest we know was a fine athlete and was particularly proud of the fact that he was a scratch golfer. He was so adept, that it was difficult to find a game and he had resorted to giving members of his parish several strokes and other advantages just to get them to play. And, despite the advantages he gave those players, he had never been beaten.

One day he decided he would use his skills to pull one of his flock closer to God. Old Mr. Donaldson had raised a family in the parish and though his wife and children attended Mass regularly, Donaldson himself had not been seen in the church for several years. It was rumored that Donaldson spent every Sunday at the racetrack and took pride in his gambling prowess.

Our priest thus presented himself at Donaldson's front door and offered the old man a wager. They would play one round of golf together and the priest would give Donaldson whatever handicap he desired to make it fair. If the priest still won, Donaldson would have to show up for Sunday Mass for at least one year. If Donaldson won, he would get to keep the priest's clubs and would not be bothered to attend Mass.

Donaldson thought about the proposition for a second and then agreed to play the priest. The only concession he asked would be that he be allowed two 'gottchas' during the match.

The priest had never heard of a 'gottcha' before but it sounded something like a 'mulligan'. Old Donaldson said he would explain exactly what 'they' were on the course and the two men shook hands on their agreement.

On the first tee Donaldson went first and hit a feeble drive that bounced along about a hundred feet. The priest could almost smell victory as he took his turn at the tee. After a few powerful back swings, he prepared to strike the ball.

In the middle of his downswing a horrendous pain struck the priest in his groin. His body crumpled and his golf ball rolled into the ditch. Grimacing in pain, the priest looked down to see Donaldson just letting go of the tight grip he had applied to the priest's testicles.

"That's one gottcha."

Donaldson smiled wickedly. The match continued. Old Donaldson never needed to use the second 'gottcha'. The priest lost by fifteen strokes while waiting for it! Donaldson still has not been back to Mass.

SPELLING

A female minister was visiting India for the first time and at a small restaurant in Calcutta she found herself seated next to a table where three Indian yogis were having a heated discussion in English. Without being rude, she tried to listen to them. The first yogi was saying,

"You must spell it the simplest way, 'w-o-o-m'."

"No," said the second, "I believe it is, 'w-o-o-m-b'."

The third replied insistently that the correct spelling would be, 'w-o-o-o-m-b-r'.

Our lady minister had heard enough. In her best attempt to be helpful and demonstrating Christian kindness, she got up and approached the men at the table saying authoritatively,

"The correct spelling is 'w-o-m-b'." And then she graciously excused herself and went back to her own table.

The three yogis looked astonished as they watched her leave.

Then the first yogi said to the other two,

"Do you suppose she is right?"

"I don't know," said the second.

The third replied that he thought the lady was just a little too young to truly know the sound of an ELEPHANT PASSING WIND.

ONE-TWO-THREE

A hard-bitten old widowed Amish farmer was driving his buggy home from church with his new, young wife Rachel beside him. The old nag pulling the carriage was kind of ornery and refused to move forward at the next road intersection. The old farmer cussed at the horse and finally said,

"That's One!"

The horse turned its head around and then proceeded ahead. At the next intersection the horse paused to visit with another horse in the pasture next to the road. The old farmer flogged at the horse with the reins and yelled,

"That's Two!"

The horse gave in and moved forward again until they reached the neighbor's flower garden. Here the horse stopped completely and proceeded to munch the neighbor's flowers. The old Amish farmer's face was beet red as he screamed,

"That's Three!"

And with that, he leaped from the seat of the old buggy, took his shotgun out from behind the seat and shot the poor horse dead on the spot. Rachel was shocked and upset by her new husband's behavior and told him,

"That was a stupid and cruel thing to do! Now how are we going to get the carriage back to the farm?"

The old farmer looked at his wife and barked,

"That'll be One, Rachel."

GREAT GURU

An aspiring Yogi in India wanted to find a guru. He searched everywhere before finding the ashram of Swami O -mi-by-gosh.

He was told that he would be accepted into the teachings of the great swami, but that he must agree to abide by the old ashram's golden rule of silence - he would not be allowed to speak a single word for ten years.

The young yogi enthusiastically agreed and was ushered into his own room at the ashram. There he meditated daily, did his daily yoga poses and kept to the rule of silence.

At the end of the ten years, the yogi was given a written instruction that he was to present himself to the swami and would be allowed to ask the master one question.

The yogi took his time walking across the compound. In his head he mulled over this opportunity before finally presenting himself to the seated swami.

"Do you have a question for me, my son?"

"Yes," said the yogi, "why are the beds here so hard?"

The swami sat there without answering and just fixed his eyes on the young yogi. Finally, one of the attendants took the yogi by the arm and led him back to his room.

Here the yogi spent another ten years contemplating his brief encounter with the great master. Again, at the end of these ten years, he received another letter asking him to bring one question to the great swami.

The yogi was getting older now and took many meaningful footsteps on the way to see the swami. Prostrating himself before the seated swami, who seemed unchanged by the passage of time, the yogi asked,

"Master, why isn't the food here cooked properly?"

Again, there was no answer and the yogi was again led back to his own quarters. There he spent ten more long years before he received a note to see the swami again.

This time, though older, the yogi marched purposefully across the ashram and bowed before the seated yogi. Without being asked a question, he simply stated,

" I Quit."

The yogi ushered himself out of the room and went back to pack his meager belongings. He was not there to hear the great Swami O-mi-by-gosh tell the attendant.

"It's about time. All he did around here was complain anyway."

THE HAIRDRESSER

A newly ordained woman minister had just been chosen to lead the congregation in the small community of Leeds, England. This church had a long history of male-ministers-only and the choice of a woman had upset some of the older, more traditional members.

One of these happened to be the town hairdresser. The new minister had heard these rumors and decided that she would seek the woman out and have her hair done before she left to visit London.

The minister found the hairdresser's salon and introduced herself while complimenting the woman on her dress and the lovely decor in her shop.

Despite the compliments, the old hairdresser's dour expression never changed. She seemed almost displeased when the minister asked if she would style her hair. The quiet in the shop felt overwhelming as the hairdresser grudgingly motioned the minister to sit in the salon chair and began to cut her hair. Finally, the hairdresser asked out of curiosity, why the minister needed her hair styled - wasn't her old cut good enough?

The minister explained that there was nothing wrong with her old style but that she was making a special trip to London this week and wanted to look her best.

The hairdresser wrinkled up her nose and said,

"London? Why would anyone want to go there? It's crowded and dirty and cold and foggy. You have to be crazy to go to London! So, how are you getting there?"

"Oh, I'm flying on Brit Air and I got such a great rate that I'll be using the savings to donate to our church Sunday School."

The hairdresser ignored the generosity and replied,

"Brit Air! That's a terrible airline. The planes are old and cramped, the flight attendants are ugly and they always arrive late. So, where are you staying in London?"

"I found a lovely inexpensive place near the British Museum called the Jenkins.'

"Ha," replied the hairdresser, "I know the place. My friend thought it would be nice too. But it's old, smelly and really a dump - probably the worse hotel in the city. So, whatcha going to London for anyway?"

"I'd like to visit Westminster Cathedral and maybe see the Queen."

"Yeah, right.... you and a million other people. You'll be lucky if she's even in town this week. You'd better be prepared for a really rotten week. You'd be better off not going."

The minister didn't know how to respond, so, she just thanked the woman politely, left a generous tip and set off to begin packing.

A month later the minister was back in town and had begun her ministry. The hairdresser was noticeably absent from the Sunday services. Rumor was, that the woman's pride and obstinateness would keep her from ever attending while a woman was in the pulpit.

The minister decided to visit the woman again at her salon. Taking a seat to get her hair done, she could see the hairdresser snickering to her other customers and pointing at the minister in derision.

When it was the minister's turn, the hairdresser asked loudly enough for the other customers to hear,

"So, how was your trip to London?"

"Oh, it was wonderful! My flight was overbooked, so they moved me to a first class seat right next to a handsome and spiritually - interested businessman. The food on the flight was wonderful and my hotel had just finished adding a brand new suite that they let me use it for the same price."

The hairdresser wrinkled up her nose and rather smugly muttered,

"That might be all well and good. But I bet you didn't get to see the Queen."

"Well, the Queen wasn't there when I first walked by Buckingham Palace. But a uniformed guard tapped me on the shoulder as I was going by and pointed to a tiny gate. I entered the gate and the Queen herself was standing there. She was handing out a special greeting and I was able to walk right up to her, get one, and even talk to her a bit."

"Reallllyyy...And what did she have to say?"

The minister smiled to herself for a brief second before answering a little more loudly,

"She said, 'Where did you get that crappy hairdo?'"

THE BULL

A Franciscan monastery was in dire financial trouble. They had a large farm and an extensive garden that surrounded the building but the monks were cash poor. The monks got together one evening and praying, came up with the idea of using their remaining cash to purchase a bull.

The monastery farm was now home to a dozen dairy cattle. But with a bull, they would be able to breed the cows and sell the calves. They were in agreement that this was a good plan. But, whom would they send on such an important mission?

Most of the monks were exceptionally busy preparing for the coming holidays. The only monks with time to spare were the newly arrived twins, Herman and Weiser. Both brothers had a great calling to God but their abilities in the world were doubted.

Herman had survived the failure of three businesses that he had tried to start before coming to the monastery and he cringed whenever anyone mentioned money - even donations.

His brother Weiser loved God, smiled a lot and spent his days sniffing the flowers in the monastery garden. Before coming to the monastery, he had lived with his brother without working and had just spent his time visiting with strangers in the nearby park.

The other monks decided they would have to trust the brothers but would try to make it simple for them. They located an ad from a farmer in the next county that offered to sell his healthy bull for $500..

Herman and Weiser were brought in and handed the $500. and the directions to the farmer's ranch. The head monk explained the importance of the mission but while he was talking, Weiser was preoccupied with a clover he was holding to his nose. Herman meanwhile, paid attention and stepped forward to take the money. He then told Weiser to stay behind while he went to get the bull.

Herman arrived at the farm with the money. The bull

looked fit and healthy but there was a small problem. The farmer would accept the agreed upon price but was not willing to deliver the bull to the monastery because his truck was broken.

Herman asked the farmer if he would accept less money for not delivering the bull but the farmer was only willing to knock one dollar off of the agreed upon price - and this was conditional upon the bull being taken away by the next day.

Herman knew that the monastery had a truck large enough to pick up the bull, but he didn't have enough time to go all the way back and get it himself. He would have to somehow get a message to his brother Weiser to bring the truck.

At the local telegraph office, Herman took out the $1 left from the sale of the bull and asked how much it would cost to send his brother the following message.

'I've bought the bull but need you to get the keys to the old monastery truck and drive it out here so that we can put the bull in it and bring it home.'

The man in the telegraph office explained that the name heading the telegram was free, but that each additional word would cost one dollar. The message, as currently worded would cost $31..

Herman started to panic. He would only be able to send one word! After much thought he finally paid for the following message:

To: BrotherWeiser....'COMFORTABLE.'

The telegraph operator sent the message, took the $1 in payment and then turned to Herman and asked how his brother would know what to do from the one word 'comfortable'.

Herman replied,

"Well my brother is a bit simple. The word is long. He'll read it very slowly... com--for--da--bull."

AERO-PLANE RIDE

The old Amish minister and his wife Rachel had just retired after serving in their small rural congregation for over fifty years. During that time they had never had time for any vacations, had watched every penny and donated any savings back to the community.

Their first big trip in retirement was to the state fair. The old minister looked on in amazement at the unusual sights, rides and people all around them. His first pension check was recently cashed and the money was in his pocket.

The biggest impression left on the old man was by a stunt pilot who flew overhead performing aerial acrobatics in the sky. The pilot ended his performance by landing on the fairgrounds next to a sign offering rides to the public.

The old minister looked at the sign, looked at his wife and said,
"I'd sure like to take me a ride in that there aero-plane."

His wife Rachel, replied,
"Yes, but the sign says it is $40. for a ride. And $40. is $40."

The old Amish man looks down dejectedly and follows his wife home.

The following year the couple returns to the fair and again the old minister sees the airplane ride sign. He says,
"Rachel, I sure do still want that aero-plane ride. If I don't do it soon, I'll soon be dead and never get the chance."

Rachel again replies,
"That there aero-plane ride still says $40.. And $40. is $40.."

The old Amish man looks down again and is about to leave. But this time the plane's pilot has heard their conversation and steps forward to approach the elderly couple.
"Listen," he says, "I'd like to make a deal with you. I'll take you both up for a ride in my airplane. And the ride will be free if you can be quiet and not say a word. But if you say anything or even scream, you'll have to pay for the ride."

The old Amish minister and his wife Rachel look at each other. Both nod their assent and the pilot helps them into the back seat of the old bi-plane. The plane takes off and the pilot goes through his entire repertoire of twists, barrel rolls and loops.

Finally the pilot lands the plane and goes to congratulate the couple for not loosing their composure and yelling in the more severe maneuvers the way most young people did.

The old man is still a bit shaky as he replies,
"Well I almost said something back in that last loop when Rachel fell out... but.... $40. is $40...."

WINDSHIELD WIPERS

A minister of German heritage was caught out in an old fashioned Oklahoma blizzard. The car he was driving was an inexpensive foreign make and its windshield wipers were having a hard time keeping up with the driving wet snow. Finally, the frail little wipers blew off completely in a powerful gust of wind.

The resourceful minister pondered for a moment. He knew he couldn't continue on without something to clear his windshield. It was getting colder by the minute and he had a very important marriage ceremony to perform in the next town.

Hopping out of the car and into the storm, the minister strode out into a field next to the road and tipped over a large flat rock. Underneath it was a pile of hibernating rattlesnakes. Grabbing two of the larger snakes, he took them back to his car and installed one each - on the two empty blade holders.

He arrived in town just in time to start the marriage ceremony. A curious guest noticed the snakes on the minister's car and asked him about them.

"Vat's the matter. You never heard of vind-chilled vipers?'

THE ENGINEER

An engineer dies and arrives at Heaven's gate. An Angel at the gate tells him that must be at the wrong place because his name is not on the list. Shaking his head, the poor man leaves and takes himself down to the gates of Hell where he welcomed.

It doesn't take long before the horrible conditions in Hell bother the engineer and he starts making some improvements. Using the limited materials in Hell, he is able to make a simple air conditioner, build a fountain and add some landscaping.

Then one-day God came to pay an unexpected visit to Satan. Looking around at the bubbling fountain, the new flower gardens and feeling the cool air flowing, God asked Satan how all this was possible.

Satan laughed and told God that with the help of the engineer, they were thinking of making some even more lavish improvements.

God looked startled as he replied,

"An engineer! There must have been a mistake. We don't send engineers to Hell. He should not be here. Send him back."

Satan just sneered and said,

"Forget it! I like having an engineer and he's staying."

God says,

"If you don't sent him back immediately - I'll sue you!"

Satan laughs again and replies,

"And just where are YOU going to find a lawyer!"

THE POLITICIAN

A crooked politician had just died after a lengthy illness. Arriving at the gate to the underworld, he is asked by the Angel at the gate whether he would prefer to enter democratic Hell or communist Hell.

Having been raised in America, the politician is about to say democratic Hell, but thinks about it twice and asks the Angel first how they differ? The Angel can't explain but says that if he is uncertain, he may visit both before deciding.

Always looking for the best deal, the politician decides to visit both. At the gates to democratic Hell he is met by Donald Trump. The politician asks Trump what democratic Hell is like.

Trump answers that in democratic Hell they are cut all over by demons with knives, salt is poured in the wounds, then they are tossed into boiling oil and ripped apart by hungry animals. They are given another body and the torture begins all over again.

The politician is shaken by the horror of this 'democratic' eternity. In desperation, he takes himself over to the gate marked communist Hell.

Outside this gate he is met by Joe Stalin. The evil old communist dictator looks terrible. The politician is afraid to ask, but does so anyway with a quavering voice,
"What's it like in there in communist Hell?"

Stalin's bruised, bleeding figure looks up mournfully and answers,
"It's terrible. They slice you with knives, salt the wounds and dip you in oil before they let the animals attack what's left. And then it starts all over again"

"But... But that sounds just like democratic Hell!"
"True," says Stalin, "but here we sometimes don't have oil, and sometimes we don't have enough knives."

FRUSTRATION

A minister, a priest and a rabbi are all having dinner together and get into a discussion about the meaning of three words: irritation, aggravation and frustration. What were the differences and which might be the most difficult to overcome?

The three decide a test is in order and the minister gets up first to present his view of 'irritation'.
He goes to the nearby pay phone, checks the phone book, places some coins in the phone, calls a local Mormon church elder and asks,
"Can I speak to James?"

A sleepy voice answers, "No, there is no one here named James," and hangs up.

"That," says the minister, "is an example of irritation."

The priest gets up next. He goes to the same phone and calls the same church elder and asks,

"Is James there?"

The voice on the other end is a little more awake this time and it solidly responds,

"There is no James here," and hangs up.

"That," says the priest, "is a man who is aggravated."

The rabbi now gets up, puts his coins in the phone and announces to his friends, "Now this is an example of frustration."
He calls the same number and asks,

"Hello, this is James. Do you have any messages for me?"

TELLING A JOKE

A new monk had recently arrived at the monastery and was preparing for bed in his tiny cell-like room. As he pulled his one blanket up to his chin, he heard the number 'Eight' shouted loudly down the corridor, followed by uproarious laughter from the other monk's rooms.

Three more numbers were shouted out and each was followed by bellowing laughs and guffaws. The new monk was curious and got up and visited the monk in the room next door.

"Brother, what are those numbers I hear being called out?"

His brother monk explained that the monks in this dormitory had been together so long, that they had memorized each other's jokes and instead of re-telling the whole thing each time, they just shouted out the number of some of their favorites.

The young monk thanked his brother monk for the new information and went back to his room. While lying there listening to more numbers being shouted and the laughter that ensued, he decided it might be fun to join in. At the next pause between 'jokes', he yelled out,

"Four!"

There was a deathly silence. So, he tried again.

"Six!"

Again, there was no response. In desperation, he decided to use a number that had previously brought a gleeful response and yelled out,

"Eight!"

There was no response at all and the joke-telling seemed to be done for the evening. The monk went to sleep perplexed by his failure to illicit any laughs from the other monks. The next day he went next door again and asked the monk there,

"Brother, why is it that no one would laugh at the numbers of the 'jokes' I called out last night?"

The other monk thought carefully for a second and then answered,

"I guess some guys just don't know how to tell a joke."

THE BURGLAR

A burglar broke into the church rectory while the priest was at Sunday Mass. Finding the house empty, he was quietly unloading the kitchen silverware into his bag when a deep voice called out,
"Jesus is watching you!"
The burglar froze in his tracks but, when silence returned, he decided to continue helping himself to the cutlery.

"Jesus is watching you!' came the voice again.

Frightened out of his wits, the man looked carefully around him. He seemed to be alone in the kitchen except for a large parrot in a cage. Looking closely at the parrot, he asked the bird if it had spoken.
The bird answered, "Yes."
Breathing a sigh of relief, the burglar asked the bird if it had a name.

"Yes," said the bird, "its Stinker."

"Stinker!' laughed the burglar. "That's a stupid name.
What jerk gave you a name like that?"

"The same jerk who named that Doberman over there 'Jesus'."

EAT RIGHT

An elderly married couple was killed in a car crash
together after celebrating their 70th Anniversary. They had lived
long and healthy lives mainly because the wife had been devoted
to fitness and proper diet for both of them.
A heavenly Angel escorted the couple to Heaven where
Saint Peter gave them both a short tour.

"This is the mansion where you will live," said Saint Peter.

It was more like a castle with vaulted ceilings and fifty
oversized rooms. Each was decorated more extravagantly than the
next, with fireplaces and a jacuzzi in each room.

"Wow," said the old man, "this is quite a place. How much is this
going to cost?"

To which Saint Peter replied,

"This is Heaven, it is free."

Strolling outside, they gazed in wonder at the beautiful
gardens surrounding their new home. The old man watched as a
golf ball flew by in the distance. He asked Saint Peter if there

was a golf course nearby.

"Yes," said Saint Peter. "There are two championship golf courses that back right up to your property."

"Whew," wheezed the old man. "And what are their green fees like?'

Saint Peter answered,
"This is Heaven. They are free."

Walking over to the nearest course clubhouse, the couple marveled at the enormous array of delicious cooked foods adorning the many tables inside.
"That's quite a spread!" said the man. "How much to eat?"

"I don't think you quite understand yet," said Saint Peter, "this is Heaven. Everything is free. And beside that, you can eat as much as you want of anything you want and you will never get fat or sick."

For some reason the old man got upset at this. He threw his hat down on the floor and stomped on it angrily. Spitting on the floor, he shrieked at his wife to leave him alone. Saint Peter tried to help his wife calm the old man down.

"What's wrong? Is there something about Heaven you don't like?"

The old man was still fuming, but he managed to fix a baleful stare at his wife as he yelled,

"It's all your fault. You and your stinking bran muffins!
If it hadn't been for them, I know I could have been here twenty years ago!"

TWINS

A pregnant young Italian woman was being rushed to the hospital by her husband. On the way The car went out of control and rolled down a cliff killing the husband and seriously injuring the young woman who was taken away by ambulance.

At the hospital the doctors delivered a set of twins, a boy and a girl, successfully while the young mother remained in a deep coma.

Six months went by before the young mother was finally revived, opened her eyes and asked what had happened.

The doctor explained that her husband was gone but her twin babies had been delivered successfully. They were healthy and were living with her single, younger brother.

As soon as the woman was able, she left the hospital to retrieve her children from her younger brother who lived nearby in a bachelor pad with his comedian buddies.

At her brother's apartment a nun answered the door while holding one of the twins in each arm. The young mother cried joyfully as she took her twins into her arms for the first time.

Her young daughter looked adoringly up into her face and the nun explained that the girl had been baptized while she was in the hospital and her brother had named her, 'Denise'.

The young mother nodded approvingly. Her concerns for her younger brother as a proper parent disappearing as she asked the nun if her son had also been baptized.

The nun hesitated a bit before replying that he had indeed been baptized at the same time and was now known to all as,
'Denephew'.

BRIBERY

A married woman was nearly caught with her lover when her husband came home from work early. Looking around in a panic, she hid her lover in the pantry closet. The lover thought he was alone until the unmistakable sound of breathing was heard behind him.

In the dim closet light, the lover was relieved to see that it was only the woman's young son. The little boy looked up at the lover and asked,

"It's awfully dark in here, isn't it mister?"

The lover tried to hush the boy and handed him $10 to stay quiet. But the little boy shook his head and said,

"That's not enuf."

The lover dipped into his pocket and handed the boy another $10. But the little boy replied,

"Still not enuf."

The lover pulled out his last $20 and handed it to the boy. The boy looked at the cash in his hand and nodded that he would be quiet.

The next day, the mother took her young son to the store and was shocked when she caught him pulling ten-dollar bills out of his pocket to buy candy. She asked where the money had come from but her son wasn't talking. Finally she grabbed him by the hand and pulled him out of the store saying,

"If you won't tell me, you'd better tell Father O'Reilly, or you'll go to hell with the rest of the bad boys."

The mother drove them directly to the Catholic Church and put her young son in the line waiting to make confessions. The boy was terrified as he had never been to confession before. As his turn came to enter the confessional, he turned with pleading eyes back to his mother. But she angrily waved him to enter.

Inside the dimly lit confessional, the boy looked at the shadow of the priest sitting on the other side listening. He wasn't sure how to begin, so he just said,

"It's awfully dark in here, isn't it?

To which the shadow figure on the other side of the curtain sharply replied,

"Don't start with me again!"

BACHELORS

A pair of very shy, elderly bachelors died and went to Heaven. Saint Peter met them at the gate and informed them that although they had lived exemplary lives and would be welcomed into Heaven, there was a small problem.

Heaven was now full. A new addition was being added and the Angels were hard at work preparing it. But, it wouldn't be ready for at least another week.

Until then, they and everyone else who passed on would be given an unusual opportunity to return to Earth for that week. But, because their old bodies had been disposed of, they would have to choose other forms in which to reside.

After a little thought, the first shy guy asks to go back to Earth as an eagle where he could fly high above nature and live freely in the wild.

"It is done," says Saint Peter, and the Angels whisk the first man back to Earth to live as an eagle.

The second shy guy thinks a little longer and asks Saint Peter if anything that he does during this week on Earth will be held against him when it is time to return to Heaven.

"No," says Saint Peter, "you have already earned your way into Heaven. Nothing you do this week will be held against you."

"Well then," he stammers a little bit, "If it doesn't matter, I've been a bit shy and lonely and feel I've missed out on a lot of things. Could I return to Earth as a young stud?"

"It is done," says Saint Peter, and the Angels take the man back to Earth.

The week goes by quickly and Heaven's new addition is ready and open. Saint Peter calls his Angels together and asks them to return all the souls who have been hanging out in other forms on Earth.

The next day all the souls have been returned except one. Saint Peter asks who is still missing,

"Was it that one who wanted to be an eagle?'

"No," said the head Angel, "that one was easy. He was just hanging around with the other eagles on the mountaintop."

"Well, who then?"

" It is that bachelor friend of his. The young stud."

"And where is he?'

"The best we can figure out - in Canada somewhere - on a snow tire."

THE TEST

A young southern boy was drowned while swimming in a creek. He was met at the heavenly gates by Saint Peter. Saint Peter explained that because the boy was still young, he had not yet earned a place in Heaven. He would still be given a chance to get in by taking a short test.

The boy said he would do his best, but hoped it wasn't too hard, because book learning wasn't his strong suit.

There are just three questions said Saint Peter and we adjust them for your age. Answer them correctly and you will spend eternity in Heaven.
The first is,

"How many days of the week start with the letter 't'?"

The boy thought for a bit before answering,

"Two - today and tomorrow."

Saint Peter was surprised by the answer but, even though it wasn't what he expected, it too, was correct.

"How about this one? How many seconds are there in a year?"
This was a much tougher question and the boy took some time before delivering his answer.

"Twelve. JAN2cd, Feb2cd, March2cd, April2cd............"

Saint Peter shook his silver-bearded head. Again, it wasn't what was expected, but the boy did have a point.

"Okay," said Saint Peter, "I'm giving you credit for that one as well. Answer this last question right and you will join us in Heaven."

"What is God's first name?"

Without much thought, the young boy answered,

"Harold is God's first name."

Taken aback, Saint Peter asks the boy why he thought God's first name is 'Harold'?

"Gosh, everybody knows that. It's in the prayer."

"And which prayer is that?"

"The Lord's Prayer of course..."

"Our Father who art in Heaven, Harold be thy name."

THE MURDERER

The old Anglican bishop lived alone in retirement in the countryside. His only son, Reggie had lived with the bishop but had been recently taken away to prison for murdering his employer. The disheartened bishop decided to put in a small garden to bring some color and cheer to his solitary life.

But as he tried to dig, he found the ground too hard and full of rocks to deal with in his frail condition. The old man wrote to his son in prison:

"Dear Reggie,
I miss you so much. I tried to put in a flower garden today to remind me of your cheerful company. Alas, the ground is too hard and I will have to remember you in other ways.
Love Dad."

A few days later he received a return note from his son.

"Dear Dad,
Please don't dig in the backyard! The other bodies are buried there!
Love Reggie."

That night at midnight, the prison warden, the coroner and the police arrived together. Without even speaking to the old bishop, they pushed past him and proceeded into the back yard with picks and shovels. Four hours later they muttered a brief apology on their way out.

The next day the bishop received a second letter from his son.
"Dear Dad,
Sorry I couldn't help you with the garden, but this was the best I could do under the circumstances. Hope you enjoy putting in the flowers.
Love Reggie."

AMISH ELEVATOR

An Amish boy went to the new regional shopping center for the first time with his father. All the wonderful new and unusual things they found there amazed them. In particular, they were puzzled by a set of shiny metal doors that kept opening and then closing by themselves.

The child asked,

"What are these, father?"

The father had never seen anything like them before either and told his son,

"I don't know."

As the two of them stood there pondering the meaning of the doors, a heavy older woman in a wheelchair pushed the button on the wall, wheeled herself through the open shiny doors and disappeared as the doors closed after her.

Circular numbers above the doors lit up as they watched. They noticed the numbers seem to stop and then light up in reverse order. The doors opened again in front of them and a beautiful young blonde woman stepped out from behind the doors and briskly walked away from the two staring men.

The father continued to follow the young woman with his eyes as he turned to whisper to his son.

"Go get thee thy ... mother!"

COPIES

An older Catholic monk had recently arrived at an old mountaintop monastery near Jerusalem. He had been assigned to help the monsignor in a project to make copies of some of the original church canons and laws that had been stored there.

He entered the large church hall to begin work the next day and finds dozens of other monks also making copies. He joins his brothers and makes diligent copies all day long. But, he notices in doing so, that the copies they are making are from what appears to be a copy and not an original.

This bothers the monk and that evening he seeks out the monsignor and points out what he has seen. The monsignor nods his head in approval at the monk's powers of observation. He explains that they have been making copies like this for centuries without a problem. But, if it were bothering the monk, he would find the original manuscript for him.

Satisfied that he has been listened to, the old monk returns to his quarters. The next day he continues to make copies. At supper that night, the monsignor is visibly absent. Worried, the monk looks for him. The monsignor's room is empty.

Lighting a candle, the monk opens the ancient doors leading to the basement where the church archives are kept. Taking one moss-covered stone step down at a time, the monk hears what sounds to be a dull 'thudding'.

Ahead, in the dim light of another candle, he sees the monsignor. The man's head is bloody and badly bruised. Yet as he watched, the monsignor continues to crash his damaged head against the nearby wall. It happens again and again and the man is crying in deep anguish.

The old monk rushes to the monsignor's side and cradling him gently in his arms, asks what is wrong?

Through tear-stained eyes the monsignor manages to croak out,
"The original directive to our priests, the word was CELEBRATE."

GOT RELIGION

A young missionary was living with the Inuit (Eskimo) people in northern Alaska. He was doing his best to fit in with their different life-style. So, as the Eskimo hunters were leaving for an overnight hunting expedition in a distant forest, he asked if he could join them as an observer.

They reluctantly agreed to let him come. He got dressed warmly and joined the group as it left for the forest. The group hunted all day with no luck and was beginning to believe the new missionary was to blame.

Later, as the missionary walked away from the group to answer nature's call, he returned to find the group had left without him. Panicking, the young man called out for his companions.

The hollow echo of his own voice filled him with dread as he noticed the sky starting to darken a bit. Then, in the dusk, he saw a bulky figure approaching. Rushing toward the form, he stopped in his tracks. It was a mammoth brown bear!

Turning on his heels, the young missionary ran for his life. But, no matter how hard he ran, the bear kept getting closer. Finally, exhausted and unable to continue, the missionary threw himself to his knees and pressing his palms together skyward, he implored his Heavenly father to,
"Please convert this wild animal's beastly appetites and give it some religion."

The sky darkened further as the bear came to an abrupt halt in front of the young man. Lighting flashed around them and the great beast looked confused. Then, with its paws extended skyward, it spoke in an almost pious manner,

"Thank you God... for the food I am about to receive."

EGGS

A minister was getting dressed one day and happened upon a hidden bag behind his dresser. Inside he found three eggs and over a hundred dollars in currency. He called to his wife and asked her about his find.

The wife explained in embarrassment, that she had been secretly keeping the bag throughout their marriage. She had not wanted to hurt his feelings. But it had been her custom to place an intact egg in the bag every time her husband had delivered a poor sermon.

The minister reflected for a second and thought,

"Hmmmm! Three bad sermons in over twenty years. Not bad!"

Then he asked,

"And what about all the cash?"

Her response,

"Each time I got a dozen eggs, I sold them to the neighbors for a buck."

GOD'S PICTURE

A Sunday School teacher was having her young students work on art projects for display at the church's annual Christmas celebration. One boy was drawing a reindeer. Another drawing a Santa Claus. A third, a Christmas tree.

But then she got to Reggie, who, had often been a bit of a problem in the past. His hand was busy making swirls of color across his paper. The curious teacher asked what he was drawing?

Reggie replied,

" I'm drawing God."

"Oh!" replied the teacher. "But Reggie, no one knows what God looks like."

Reggie, undaunted and not even bothering to look up from his drawing responded,

"They will in a minute, Teach!"

PAINTING THE PORCH

Elmo was a mute monk who seemed to get the least respect at the monastery. Some considered him dim -witted, others just lazy. But the bishop felt a deep piety lurked behind Elmo's silent goofy grin and general clueless -ness.
To test his belief in the monk, the bishop brought Elmo into his office and explained that the monastery would be responsible for raising more money each year to support itself. He expected Elmo to help in these efforts and believed some success might change other's opinions about the young monk.
Elmo drooled a little from the corner of his mouth and shook his head up and down indicating he understood the bishop.

"Fine, good man," said the bishop and he handed Elmo a stack of leaflets to distribute door to door in the neighboring town to solicit funds. All he had to do was hand them out and bring back any donations.
Elmo set out enthusiastically, leaflets under his arm, toward the nearby town. That evening Elmo returned to the bishop's office looking much the worse for wear. He presented himself to the bishop with his robe rumpled and a look of despair

71

on his face.

"Oh no," thought the bishop.

Directing the tired - looking monk to a chair in his office, the bishop asked Elmo how much money he had taken in for the church? Elmo looked up sadly and handed the bishop a note.

"Lost flyers. No money."

His confidence in the little monk shaken, the bishop asked,

"Well was there anything you did accomplish today? You were gone for a very long time."

Elmo's demeanor changed and a small smile grew on his face as he plunged his hand into the creases of his disheveled robe. From a deep fold in the garment, he extricated a rumpled piece of paper. Smoothing it out, he handed it enthusiastically to the bishop. On it the bishop read:

'Help wanted at Sven's Nursery. Must be able to paint.'

The bishop nodded his head. Serving takes many forms and perhaps this would be Elmo's way of contributing. But first he wanted to make sure Elmo would do a good job and not tarnish the monastery's good reputation in the community.

The bishop excused Elmo and then sought out some of the other monks who knew the man's capabilities better. The bishop was reassured that, though slow, Elmo had painted before and had done a wonderful job on his own room and on the church -dining hall.

The next day Elmo was sent back into town to take the job at Sven's nursery. Sven was a big hulking man and he looked down warily at the small monk. After a quick appraisal, Sven handed Elmo the paintbrushes and a gallon of paint.

"Here," he said, "take these and paint the porch in back of the house. Come see me when you're finished!"

A few hours later, the little monk was back at Sven's front door. Sven was a bit surprised at how quickly the monk had worked.

"Finished all ready? Did you do a good job?"

Elmo scribbled out a quick note in response. It read,

"Yes, and since I even had paint left over, I gave it a second coat."

Duly impressed, Sven reached into his thick wallet and pulled out a hundred dollar bill and handed it to the little monk.
The bishop was waiting for all the monks to turn in their collections that evening and ushered Elmo into his office upon his return. Elmo handed the bishop the hundred-dollar bill and with a happy smile left to join the other monks at supper.
The bishop looked at the hundred dollars in his hands, smiled and was about to put it away with the other church funds when he heard a loud pounding at his back door. The housekeeper had gone home, so the bishop answered it himself.
Sven stood at the door towering over the bishop with a look of red-faced rage covering his face. The bishop invited the angry man in and asked what was the matter.
Sven ripped a piece of paper out of his pocket and threw it down in front of the bishop saying only that he had found it attached to his car's windshield wiper. The bishop put on his reading glasses and immediately recognized Elmo's handwriting,

"Thanks for the job. But it's not a Porch, it's a Mercedes."

TELEPHONE POLES

After the debacle with Sven, the bishop had decided to keep Elmo on the monastery grounds where he could stay out of trouble. It was with a little bit of trepidation that the bishop allowed Elmo to continue working with the other monks.

One day there was a note from the telephone company. The monastery would receive their own free phone service if the monks could provide telephone poles on which the phone wires could be strung. Twenty poles must be installed and be ready by the next day.

The bishop re-reads the letter - the next day! The only monks available for the job were Elmo and Peter. The bishop called them both in and described how important it was that the poles be installed immediately. Then, he gave each monk a hole - borer and ten poles to install by that evening.

It was late that evening when Peter returned to say that his ten poles were installed and were ready to be wired. Shortly after that Elmo arrived looking even more tired and dirty than Peter. The bishop asked him how many poles he had installed. Silently, Elmo jotted a figure on a paper and handed it to the bishop.

"Four? This must be wrong Elmo. You know that you had to install all ten. Peter got back before you and he completed his ten. What happened to you?"

Elmo looked at the bishop and began writing another note. It simply said,

"Yes. Peter did ten, but, look at how much he left sticking out of the ground!"

HOW ARE YOU

Then there was a monk named Brother Edgy who was sent by the monastery to pick up a cow that the order had recently purchased. The money had been paid and all Edgy had to do was let the farmer put the cow in the back of a livestock truck and Edgy would drive the animal back to the monastery where the rest of the monks could help with the unloading.

The loading went well, but on the way back to the monastery, a large big rig truck drove past Edgy and forced him off the road and into a ditch. The bishop and his fellow monks waited for Edgy to return all afternoon.

Just before the monastery bell rang to announce the evening prayers, Brother Edgy appeared at the side door of the monastery. His body was covered in dirt and dried blood and he passed out before he could say a single word.

The bishop called an ambulance and Edgy was rushed to a nearby hospital where he remained in intensive care for three days. The cost of Edgy's medical care would be over a thousand dollars. But the good news was that young monk was expected to recover completely.

While Brother Edgy remained at the hospital, the bishop received a report in the mail from the county sheriff who had happened upon the accident right after it occurred. The report said that the officer on the scene had stated that the driver of the vehicle was – NOT INJURED.

The next day the bishop took the report with him to the hospital. Entering Edgy's room, the bishop took a seat next to the young monk's bed. Brother Edgy looked up, obviously happy to see his visitor.

The bishop asked Edgy if he remembered what had happened the day of the accident.

Brother Edgy started to explain,

"Yes bishop, I was helping the farmer load the ..."

"No Brother Edgy, I want to know about the accident."

"Sure bishop. There was this big truck.. And it was behind me... and then beside..."

"No," interrupted the bishop again. "Tell me what happened after the big truck left. Did a sheriff come by and talk to you?"

"Yes bishop."

"Did you tell the sheriff that you were 'fine'"?

"Yes bishop."

"But Brother Edgy, you obviously weren't fine were you?'

"No...."

"So, did you lie to the sheriff?'

"Well.... I guess I kind of did."

"What do you mean kind of? You lied, correct?"

"I'm sorry bishop. But when that sheriff came by, we heard the poor cow mooing horribly. She was hurt pretty bad. So, the sheriff took out his gun, placed it next to her head and shot her dead. Then he came over to where I was laying in the ditch and asked me,

'How are you doing?'

I looked up at that big gun … and told him as definitely as I could... 'I'M FINE."

THE OLD SINNER

An old bearded man totters on his cane quietly into the Saturday night confessional at Saint Joseph's church. Taking a seat in the confessional booth next to the priest, he begins to speak slowly,

"Father, I'll be eighty years old later this week. I have a wonderful wife at home. We've been married sixty years and have five wonderful kids and twenty healthy grandchildren. Last week I went fishing by myself and there were four college girls camping nearby.

I introduced myself to them and they invited me to stay at their campsite. That night I made love to all four of the girls and in the morning when I left they thanked me for the experience."

The priest harrumphed at this last part before speaking,

"You know it doesn't matter if the girls were willing. It is still a sin. Are you sorry for your sins?"

"What sins?"

"What do you mean 'what sins'? What kind of Catholic are you?"

"What kind of Catholic? I'm not Catholic at all. I'm a Presbyterian."

"Then why are you in here telling me all this?"

The old man smiled and said,

"Because, I'm telling everybody!"

BAPTIST BRA

A minister sheepishly walks into the lingerie department of a large store and asks the lady behind the counter for a 'Baptist Bra' for his wife in size 38D.

The sales lady looks at him closely and makes him repeat his request.

"A Baptist bra for my wife - Size 38D Please?"

The sales woman looks at him appraisingly and replies,

"We've never gotten any requests for Baptist bras. I have helped people with Catholic, Presbyterian and Salvation Army bras. Are you sure you don't want one of those?'

"No," the man replied, "It has to be a Baptist bra. But what are those other bras like?"

"Well," explained the woman, "the Catholic bra 'supports the masses'. The Presbyterian bra keeps them 'staunch and upright.' The Salvation Army bra 'lifts the downfallen. But I have never heard of the Baptist bra. Does it do anything special?"

The little minister coughed nervously before explaining that the Baptist Bra,

"Makes mountains out of molehills."

THE POPE'S HEALTH

The Pope was elderly and in poor health. One night he was admitted to the Vatican hospital where each of the cardinals who might succeed him as the next Pope was called in for an individual audience.

The Pope prayed with each of these men in turn and confided in each some of the difficulties and responsibilities of the position.

Finally there was only one cardinal left - Cardinal Guido. Guido had tears in his eyes as he knelt next to the Pope and the two men prayed. The Pope's breath became more labored, but he endured as his words came out with difficulty.

"Guido... you have been very faithful... very ambitious.... very strong... I...must..ask...you... one ...favor....

"Yes, your holiness.... Ask whatever you wish."

"Guido...Please...get...your....damn....foot...off...of...my ...oxygen....hose..!

THE PARACHUTE

Three rabbis were on vacation together and decided to take a 'walk on the wild side' and to try something 'different'. One of them suggested visiting a nightclub but the other two mentioned the 'shame' if they were found out.

The second suggested going to a spa but the other two had reservations about disrobing in public. The third rabbi came up with the idea of going skydiving. The rabbis waited for a reason not to go but, when there was no practical objection put forth, they agreed to drive to the airport together in the morning.

The next day all three rabbis were issued parachutes and given some elementary instruction on how to parachute dive safely. Then, the rabbis were flown high into the sky where the first rabbi leapt from the plane yelling,

"Jehovah!"

The second rabbi jumped into the air behind the first and the third swallowed deeply and stepped from the plane. The first rabbi's chute billowed below them. Both the falling rabbis pulled their ripcords together.

One opened, one didn't and the third rabbi crashed to his death in a cow pasture. The two remaining rabbis took their friend's remains back home. The rabbi was buried next to his synagogue. His tombstone simply read the cause of his demise as,

'Jumped to a conclusion.'

ALL IN THE FAMILY

The young minister and his wife had hired a Mexican girl named Carlotta to be their housekeeper. The girl seemed diligent and they were happy with the job she was doing. Then one day Carlotta came to the minister's wife and said she had to leave.

"But why Carlotta? Aren't you happy here?"

"Yes. But I am in the family way."

Taken aback, the minister's wife exclaimed,

"It can't be. Who is it? Who did such a terrible thing?"

"Your husband and your oldest son."

"My husband.... and my son..."

The minister's wife was crushed. How could these things have happened in her house? She gathered her courage and asked Carlotta to explain further. Carlotta continued,

"First I go into patio to clean, but your husband there and he say,
'Go. You are in my way.'

So then I go to living room to clean but your son there and he say,
'Go. You are in my way.'

So now I go because I am too much in family way."

MEMORIES

An American Indian tribal shaman was known far and wide for his grasp of deep spiritual truths and for his seemingly psychic ability to know almost everything that had ever happened.

A deeply skeptical Protestant minister decided he would visit the ancient shaman and decide for himself whether the man was truly holy or just a big fraud.

Finding the old shaman sitting on his buffalo rug, there were lines of people waiting their turns to each ask one question. The minister got in line and when it was his turn, he asked, "Can you tell me what I had for lunch eight years ago - on January 14th to be specific?"

The old man immediately answered,

"Hamburger. Next please."

The minister was a bit perplexed and put off. He didn't remember exactly himself what he had eaten that particular day but anybody could have guessed hamburger and would have had a good chance of being right.

So, the minister went back to his congregation and he denounced the old shaman as just another big fraud. Three years went by and the minister was driving by the old shaman's village. He decided to stop in and see if the old man was still there.

Sure enough, the old shaman still sat on his buffalo robe at the edge of the village. There were no longer any lines of people waiting, so the minister walked over to the shaman and greeted him with his hand in the air saying,
"How."

To which the old shaman replied,

"Medium rare with a side of curly fries, cole slaw and a chocolate shake. Next please."

CAKE

A very proper Muslim Ayatollah went into a bakery in Damascus. He asked the baker to prepare him a white almond cake in the form of an Arabic script 'g'.

The baker said that he could do this but that it would need to be done in many shaped pans and then the smaller cakes put together and iced. The entire project would take about three days.

The Ayatollah agreed to wait and would return in three days. Three days later the Ayatollah returned and the baker triumphantly showed him the beautifully gilded white almond cake in the form of a 'g'.

"Ah," said the Ayatollah, it is indeed a thing of beauty, but there has been a misunderstanding. My order was for a cake in the form of an Arabic script 'g'. And this cake is in the form of a block letter 'g'. It is not acceptable."

The crest-fallen baker looked sadly at his creation as the Ayatollah slowly dumped it into the garbage can. The baker recovered quickly and said that if the Ayatollah could wait three more days, he would prepare another cake exactly as ordered. The Ayatollah agreed to wait three more days and then departed.

Three days later the Ayatollah returned to the bakers shop. On the counter stood a beautifully decorated white almond cake in the form of an Arabic script 'g'.

The Ayatollah inspected the cake carefully and then pronounced it acceptable, "Exactly as I ordered it."

The proud baker asked if the Ayatollah would like to take the cake with him or have it delivered to his house.

"Don't bother," said the Ayatollah. "I'll just take out my fork and eat it here."

FIDELITY

A car carrying three married ministers on their way home from a church conference was destroyed in a terrible accident and there were no survivors.

All three men arrived together at Heaven's gate. Saint Peter took the first man aside and asked him how many times he had cheated on his wife during their lives together. The man proudly answered,

"None."

Saint Peter handed the man the keys to a brand new Cadillac to drive around in Heaven. Then Saint Peter turns to the next man and asks him the same question.
The man responds with a bit of guilt,

"Just once."

Saint Peter hands this man the keys to a golf cart to drive around in Heaven. Then he turns his attention to the third man who is shifting nervously and asks the question again. The man answers honestly,

"About a dozen times."

Saint Peter pierces the man with a fierce look and hands him a broken old bicycle for his transport in Heaven.

The man with the bicycle tries to get it working and begins pumping away at the pedals to get through the gate before anyone changes their mind.

Once inside the gate, the man on the bike passes the man in the Cadillac. The car is motionless on the side of the road and the man is inside sobbing his eyes out. The man on the bike stops to ask what was the matter. All the man in the Cadillac could say was,

"I just passed my wife on the road and.... She was walking..."

METEOR

The world's top scientists received information from the U.S. space telescope that a large meteor would strike the earth in less than a month. The resulting collision would send tidal waves in every direction and the polar ice caps would melt covering the entire surface of the Earth with water.

To prepare the people of the world for this unimaginable disaster, spiritual leaders from all of the great religions were asked to speak on worldwide television to their faithful.

The first night the Dalai Lama spoke about trusting in the Divine and holding no attachments to the material world.

The second night the Pope talked about confessing one's sins and preparing to enter the heavenly realm.

The third night Billy Graham spoke about it not being too late to accept Jesus as your savior.

The fourth night the chief Jewish Rabbi spoke and explained to his people that they had about thirty days left to learn to live underwater.

THE TEXAS FARMER

A prominent Texan and his wife were on a vacation and driving across the eastern United States. Late one day he stopped his big S.U.V. outside a small Amish farm in Pennsylvania. The bearded Amish farmer saw the huge S.U.V. outside and went out to invite the two strangers in for something to eat.

After a delicious dinner the Texan complimented the Amish farmer on the quality of the food served by his wife. He also mentioned that he too, was a farmer and was curious about how large the Amish farmer's 'spread' that produced this great food might be.

The Amish farmer scratched his head and replied that his

farm was about five hundred yards deep and about the same in width. Then to be polite, he asked the tall Texan about the size of his farm.

"Well," said the Texan, puffing up mightily and hitching-up his belt, "I wake up in the morning and after a good breakfast, I jump on my favorite horse and ride all day - and at the end of the day I finally reach the edge of my farm."

To this the Amish farmer nodded knowingly and said, "Yes, I know. I used to have a horse like that too..."

CLOCK SHOP

A very proper lady minister was visiting Israel for the first time. She was in the middle of her visit when she realized that her wristwatch had stopped working. Running late, She almost missed the bus with the rest of her tour group as it left for Jerusalem.

When they arrived in the Holy City, she went off to get her watch fixed. Walking down the busy streets alone and not able to read any of the signs, she was pleasantly surprised to find a little shop with several clocks in it's front window.

Entering the little shop, she approached a small -wizened man seated next to a desk.

"Excuse me sir, could you help me?"

"Yes Miss. I speak a little English. How can I help you?"

"Oh wonderful!" she exclaimed. "My watch is broken. Can you fix it for me?"

"I'm sorry Miss. I don't fix watches. I am a moyl and I perform circumcisions on young boys and men.'

"But.... But if you don't fix watches.... why do you have all those clocks in your front window?"

"Miss, what would you suggest I put out there instead?"

LIMOUSINE

The Pope was making his first visit to the United States. A huge limousine was waiting for him at the airport. The driver held the passenger door open for His Eminence.

The Pope hesitated before getting in and pulled the driver aside. He asked that as a special favor, he, the Pope, would like to drive the shiny white limo for a few blocks. The driver resisted, but finally it was difficult to say no to the Pope. Taking off his driver's cap, he placed it on the Pope's head and got in the back to give the Pope directions to the hotel.

The Pope pulled the visor of the cap down over his eyes, got behind the wheel and started the engine. Like a small boy, he giggled as the powerful engine roared. Placing the car in drive they took off heading for the Pope's hotel.

Two blocks later a policeman pulled over the large limo as it raced through an intersection without stopping. The officer looks in the driver's window and heads back to his patrol car without writing a ticket or saying a word.

Instead, he calls for dispatch and asks to speak to the captain on duty.

"Captain? Were you expecting any important visitors to the city today?"

"No. Not that I know of...Why did you pull over someone important?"

"I think so."

"Is it the governor? Someone else stopped him last week."

"No, more important than that."

"Not a senator or... my God. You didn't pull over the president did you?"

"No, not the president... but someone even more important."

"More important than the president? Just whom did you pull over?"

"I'm not sure exactly. But I do know he has the Pope as a chauffeur."

WISDOM OF SOLOMON

Two young rabbis had recently graduated from the same college. They were traveling back to their hometown to get married. They discussed in the plane together some of their thoughts about married life.

As the responsibilities of marriage were mentioned, they both realized that there would be some loss of their personal freedom. While waiting for their baggage at the airport, one of the rabbis hugged his classmate and said good-bye. He had changed his mind and was going to take the next plane to Israel.

The remaining rabbi bid his friend good-bye and good luck. He then got his bags and found a cab headed for the town's temple where the two prospective brides were waiting with their families.

There was some shock at the temple when only one rabbi emerged from the cab. After hearing about the cold feet of the man's friend, the two brides, one a blonde, the other a brunette, began to fight over who should get to marry the remaining rabbi. Even their families were feuding and before the disagreement could come to blows, the chief rabbi emerged to take the families aside.

The chief rabbi said that he would make the decision about which bride and which family would be the most 'real' for the remaining rabbi's spiritual journey into family life. But after asking several questions of both families, they seemed equally matched.

In his wisdom, the chief rabbi said that the only answer would be to cut the young rabbi in half and give half to each of the prospective brides.

"Yeah," said the mother of the brunette, "go ahead and cut the boy in half!"

The blonde's family was too stunned to say anything.

The chief rabbi then took the young rabbi by the shoulders and moved him over to the family of the brunette saying,

" Here you have found a 'real' mother-in-law."

THE DIME

An unlucky man had gambled away all of his money. He had nothing to eat and only the clothes on his back. To make matters even worse, he had to use the bathroom desperately and the only restroom in the hotel had a pay toilet.

A visiting minister saw the distraught-looking man in the hotel lobby and asked him what the problem was. The man explained his dire need and the minister handed him a dime for the toilet.

The man thanked the minister and rushed off to the bathroom. There he found the stall unlocked and after attending to his 'business', decided to return to the hotel casino and used the dime in his hand on a slot machine.

It must have been a lucky dime because he hit an immediate jackpot. The man took his winnings to the blackjack table and proceeded to win a sum of a little over a million dollars.

A local newspaper heard about the man's story and wrote an article in the local paper about this amazing change of luck. With the story was the now-lucky man's offer to split his enormous winnings with his unknown benefactor.

The minister who had lent the man the dime read the story and realized that this must be God's answer to the needed funds for their church orphanage's new roof!

The next day the minister showed up at the address of the lucky man as it was listed in the paper. Knocking on the door, the minister waited patiently. Finally, the door opened. The now-lucky man opened it himself and looked at the minister.

"What do you want?'

"Don't you remember me? I'm the man who gave you the dime."

"Oh yeah. But you're not the right one.'

"What do you mean 'the right one'?"

"Well, thanks for the dime. But I'm looking for the guy who left the stall open."

TAKING IT WITH YOU

A famous and wealthy man was near death from a terminal illness. He was preparing to die and leave his decaying body but was not so willing to leave the massive riches he had earned and still not spent. So, he began to fervently pray that he be allowed to take some of his riches with him into the afterlife.

The man's Guardian Angel heard the man's prayers and decided to intervene with God on the rich man's behalf. Finding

God in a benevolent mood, the Angel explained that the rich man had lived a good life and, though still erroneously attached to his material wealth, it would be a great comfort and a generous thing to allow the man to bring some things with him into Heaven.

God considered the Angel's request and decided to grant permission for the man to bring with him one trunk full of those things that mattered to him most.

That night as the rich man slept, the Angel appeared to him and conveyed an image of God's willingness to permit the man one trunk full of his most cherished possessions.

The rich man woke the next morning with his body racked with pain but with the memory of the Angel's promise still in place. Sensing his own imminent demise, he hurriedly phoned his bank and ordered that a trunk full of gold bars be delivered to him that same day.

The rich man was barely breathing when the trunk full of gold arrived. The next thing he knew was the feeling of his soul leaving the body but, securely in his hand was the strap attached to the heavy trunk.

The rich man then saw the gates of Heaven. Angels flowed ethereally in and out of the jeweled gates. A tall elderly, Light Being with a flowing beard stood at the gate. The rich man approached the gatekeeper and asked if this was Heaven.

The bearded Light Being explained that yes, this was Heaven and that he was expected. But, looking at the heavy trunk next to the man, said that no material possessions could be brought inside.

The rich man's face soured over and he tried to explain that an Angel had appeared to him and that God himself had given permission to bring in this one trunk. The bearded gatekeeper looked dubious about this story but picked up a golden phone and after a quick conversation, apologized to the rich man.

Yes, indeed, an extraordinary exception had been made and the man could bring his trunk into Heaven with him. Tugging the trunk behind him, the rich man entered Heaven's gate.

Word that some material reminders of the world had been

brought into Heaven soon spread. Other Souls, Spirits and Angels gathered to welcome the rich man. All wanted to see what was in the trunk.

Great anticipation was felt as the rich man unlocked the trunk and displayed that which was too important to be left behind.

A shocked gasp was heard as the glistening gold bars were revealed. And then the voice of one of the Angels,

"He brought pavement?"

BREAD AND TURNIPS

In medieval Europe, an elderly hermit was starving on his drought-ridden farm. Packing up his meager belongings, he began the long trek into the nearest city. When he arrived, he was told that there was food being given away near the great cathedral,.

The hermit approached the massive doors of the cathedral and asked the florid-faced priest in the entry.

"Can I have some bread and turnips?"

No, explained the priest. The food was distributed at the cathedral only on Sundays. Since this was Tuesday, the man must wait.

The next day the hermit returned and asked,

"Can I have some bread and turnips?"

The priest was a bit perturbed, but did his best to explain that the man must wait four more days until Sunday.

The next day the hermit was again at the cathedral in front of the priest.

"Can I have some bread and turnips?"

The priest, who was also one of the officials in charge of the Spanish Inquisition, was now angry.

"No! You cannot have any bread or turnips - and if you ask me that one more time, I'll have you nailed up onto the doors as a lesson to all foolish peasants!"

The little hermit left. But, the next day he was again in front of the priest at the cathedral. The priest looked up and slammed his fist down onto his desk and seethingly asked what the hermit wanted.

"Do you have any nails?"

This caught the priest by surprise and he had to think for a second before answering,

"No, we don't have any nails. Anything else?"

"Can I have some bread and turnips?"

FUNEREAL PROCESSION

A devout, married woman was on her way home from church when she noticed a funereal procession on it's way down the center of the street. Three long black hearses were slowly rolling down the street with a solitary woman in black mourning dress right behind them.
A large Doberman Pinscher dog that was also garbed in black followed the woman. Further behind the dog trailed a long

line of women all walking with heads bent in single file.

Our churchwoman was moved by the solemnity of the group and when it momentarily paused at a red light, she seized the moment to pay her condolences to the poor widow in black. At the same time, she inquired about the long length of the procession - her husband must have been much loved.

The widow explained,
"The first hearse is for my husband. He had tried to bring two strange women home while I was gone but was attacked and killed by my dog."
"The second and third hearses are for his two mistresses. They tried to help protect my husband, but my dog sensed that they were sinners and turned on them and killed them as well."

A brief meaningful pause occurred as the two women looked into each other's hearts. Then our church lady asked softly,
"May I borrow your dog?"

"Get in Line."

HOLY MOLEY

There was a large family of moles who lived on the church grounds. The father mole, his wife and their twenty children including the youngest, little Bobby, would come out of their mole-hole every Sunday when church was in session. The entire mole family would stand together next to their hole with their little paws folded and their heads reverently bowed.

The minister of the church noticed this odd behavior and many in his congregation commented about their newest 'members'.

The minister and his congregation decided to do something special for the reverent little mole family that Christmas. They would secretly decorate the little fir tree that sat next to the mole hole in front of the church. So, on Christmas Eve, the minister and several volunteers arrived with colored lights, candy canes, sugarplums and other goodies and proceeded to decorate the little outside tree.

On Christmas morning the father mole got up early and squeezing up through the long mole tunnel to daylight, observed the wondrous sight of the dazzling little tree. Rushing back down the mole hole, he woke his family with the news.

Each of the moles rushed to their tunnel and struggled to squeeze upward past each other to see this new wonder. The father and mother mole got up first and looked in wonder at the twinkling lights. The girl moles arrived next and admired the wrapped presents and tree garlands.

The little boy moles arrived next squeezing up the crowded mole-hole except for Bobby, who was the youngest and slowest. The boy moles were especially taken by the smell and sight of the candy canes and sugarplums.

But for little Bobby mole, the only thing he would remember from that Christmas day was ....

The Molasses.

BIG LIE

A noted Indian swami was visiting England for the first time. As he took his morning walk to the park nearest to his hotel, he passed a group of young boys in an alley. The boys were bickering loudly and a small dog quivered with fright in their midst.

Fearing for the dog's safety, the swami asked the boys what they were doing. The oldest of the boys looked around sullenly and said that they had found the lost little dog and each wanted to keep him. To decide who should get to keep the dog, they had decided to award the dog to whoever who could tell the biggest lie.

They were now taking turns telling preposterous stories and deciding whose lies were greater. And, they were having trouble agreeing which ones were the worse.

The swami was visibly upset that these young men were wasting their talents in such an un-lofty pursuit and also terrifying the small dog in the process. He raised his voice and harangued the boys about the pitfalls of lying and the karmic repercussions of not telling the truth.

Gesturing wildly with his arms for emphasis, he finished by stating that he was only trying to help their souls and that in his own youth an enlightened master had wakened him to the point that he was now able to avoid any untruth.

When the swami finished speaking, the oldest of the boys sighed, looked over at his young friend, who held the puppy, and said.

"Okay, give him the dog."

NUN'S NIGHT OUT

A group of nuns had just completed their final teaching assignments for the year at the local church school. To celebrate they went to an amusement park near the ocean. Though still in their dark habits, they had a wonderful time at the beach.

That evening, after all that sun, the rides and the water, they were headed back to the bus station. Before they got there, one of the nuns realized she needed to go to the bathroom and that it wouldn't wait until they got back.

There was a small restaurant nearby and the nuns could tell there was a large party going on inside. Loud drunken voices and shrieking laughter erupted from its narrow confines. With no other place in sight open, the nuns conferred and approached the restaurant door as their sister went in to use the bathroom.

The embarrassed and terribly nervous women looked around at the boisterous revelers and as they looked, suddenly things got very quiet. The nun in-need asked a large man who seemed to be the manager if she could use his bathroom. The large florid man answered,

"It's around the corner. But I don't think you should."

"Why not?" asked the surprised nun.

"Well because there is a life-sized statue of a naked man in there. And his private parts are only covered by a fig leaf."

"That's not a problem. I'll just look the other way."

And with that, she gestured to her fellow nuns to follow her to the restroom. The group of nuns proceeded around the corner and they could hear the party returning to normal after they passed. The nuns all used the facilities as each took turns guarding their privacy at the restroom door. As they finished and were walking back through the main room, the party stopped again and the guests broke into a round of laughter and applause.

The first nun asked the manager what the applause was all about?

The laughing man handed a drink in her direction and explained that they were only laughing to express their shared kinship with their dear sisters.

"Kinship?" sputtered the nun. "What kinship do we have with a bunch of drunken sex-crazed louts and revelers like yourselves?"

"Well," said the man. "Ever since we hooked up the building's light switch to that fig leaf, we haven't had quite so gaudy a light show as we had today!"

"Now, are you so sure you wouldn't like to join us?"

SKINNY-DIPPERS

There was a large pond located on the church property in a field behind the church. It was a perfect spot for church picnics and the children from the Sunday School enjoyed the cool water when classes were done.

The young minister, who was responsible for the church budget was upset that people from town, who weren't even church members, had been using the pond, picnicking and leaving their trash behind.

The minister was tired of paying to have all the trash hauled away. He decided to wait in the bushes by the pond that evening and chase the trespassers away.

After supper, he made himself comfortable behind a large bush and settled in to wait. A full harvest moon rose and by it's ample light, he watched as five young women from the town appeared over a nearby hill carrying a picnic basket.

None of the young ladies belonged to the congregation. But their tender voices and gleeful laughter made him loath to disturb their party. He watched as they arranged their blanket and set up a beautiful picnic meal on it.

Then one suggested that a swim would be perfect before eating. First one, then another began stripping off their dresses and undergarments. The embarrassed minister turned his eyes away in modesty. Looking back, he saw that they were now all in the water.

Just then there was the loud sound of someone else approaching from behind and a large flashlight lit up the edge of the pond. It was the senior minister! The old man had sensed there was something wrong and had come down to check it out.

The women in the pond shrieked and were doing their best to cover up body parts that a swimsuit normally should have been covering. Their shrill voices called out as they moved into deeper water,

"Go away. We're not coming out until you leave!"

The old minister cackled and said that he hadn't come down to the pond to see them naked or to make them get out of the pond. And, that they were welcome to stay as long as they liked - while he was feeding - the church alligators!

The water was soon empty as the old minister cackled once more. Wiping his tired eyes, he called his young assistant out from behind the bushes and together they finished the food in the picnic basket.

RESPECT

The new minister goes into the hardware store to buy some rat poison. The counter girl asks,
"Should I wrap it up, or do you want to eat it here?"

The new minister was kidnapped while visiting the Middle East. The gunmen sent a ransom note home along with a piece of the minister's finger. The family sent it back along with a message saying - 'they needed more proof.'

The new minister came back from a visit to the circus. He bragged that they must have recognized him from church because, when he went to visit the freak show, they let him in free.

The new minister was called to the local tavern to assist one of his flock who had imbibed one too many. But he was asked to leave just as he arrived because, they didn't want to spoil the happy hour.

The new minister was taking a plane and was asked by the stewardess if he wanted any dinner. The minister asked, 'What choices are there?'
The stewardess replied, 'Yes or no.'

PATRIOTISM

The priest had decided to honor all the many members of his parish who had died in wars defending their country. He had a huge plaque made with an American flag in its center and the names of those to be remembered listed below it. This plaque he had installed in a place of honor in the foyer of the church.

The next day, which was Sunday, the priest stood in the entry and watched as all his church members filed by and each stopped to admire and pay their respects to their fine new memorial.

Little Reggie came through with his family. The young boy looked at all the names and then approached the priest asking,

"Pastor, what is this new thing?"

The priest gently explained that it was a special memorial to all the men and women who had died in the service.

To which little Reggie replied,

"Which one? The nine o'clock or the ten-thirty?"

COSSACKS

In the early days of czarist Russia, a horde of savage Cossack warriors swept boldly into a small Jewish village. Bursting into the small village temple, they drew a circle in the middle of the floor and placed Rabbi Lickstein into the middle of it. They left him there saying that, if he left the circle, they would kill him.

Outside, the Cossacks gathered all of the village women including the rabbi's wife. The women shrieked and cried for help all afternoon as the Cossacks abused and raped them. After the Cossacks had finished with the women and left for the next town, the rabbi's wife dragged herself back to the temple where her husband still stood in his circle.

"You miserable coward! Didn't you know what they were doing to us?"

Indignantly, the rabbi replied,

"How dare you call me a coward! I'll have you know that while they were with you, I stepped over their stupid circle at least three times."

GARDEN OF EDEN

God created Adam and placed him in the Garden of Eden. But Adam was sad and God asked what was the matter? Adam said he was lonely and didn't have anyone to talk to. God told him that this could be easily fixed. God would create a 'woman'. Adam was excited and wanted to know more about this thing called 'woman'.

God explained that woman would be his ever-constant companion and his helpmate. The woman would cook, clean, bear and raise his children. She would love him, console him and never nag or disagree with his plans.

Adam couldn't believe his good fortune and thanked God, asking if this great gift would cost him anything. God replied that there would only be the small cost of an arm and a leg.

To which Adam replied,

"And what can I get for a rib?"

THE MINISTER'S WIFE

The minister's wife took her husband to the doctor for his annual check-up. After an abnormally long wait, the doctor motioned the woman to join him in his office alone.

The worried wife asked if there was anything wrong. The doctor patiently explained that the minister was on the verge of a complete breakdown. And that the already-frail man would surely die unless, he got a warm healthy breakfast and at least one other nutritious meal every day.

He would also need to avoid any stressful conversations or any taxing chores. The house would also need to be kept scrupulously clean to avoid any contact with germs.

The wife thanked the doctor and returned to her husband in the waiting room. The frail minister asked his wife what the doctor had said.
Her reply,

"Sorry Honey, he said you were going to die."

IRISH DAUGHTER

A pretty, young, Irish Catholic girl went away to London to find a job as a writer. She soon began sending some money and thoughtful gifts home to her large impoverished family.

This went on for a few years until the grateful parents sent her a note asking her to return home for a visit. Her father was ill and elderly and wanted to see her.

The dutiful daughter caught the next flight back to Ireland. She appeared the next day at the family home as she stepped out of a chauffeur-driven Rolls Royce. She wore beautiful designer clothes, expensive jewelry and her hair was elegantly styled.

Her elderly father and mother greeted her at the door. Both were happy to see her, but both had wondered at how quickly their daughter had found success in such a strange place as England.

As if reading their thoughts, their daughter spoke first.

"Mom, Dad, I've been meaning to tell you something for a while. I can't hide the truth from you any longer and the guilt is killing me. I wasn't able to find a job as a writer so instead I became a prostitute."

Her elderly father moaned loudly, grasped his chest and

collapsed. An ambulance was called and he was whisked away to the hospital. There he remained on life support for many days. When it appeared that he had lost his will to live, a priest was called to administer the Last Rites.

When the priest had finished, his daughter went to his side and wept. The old man's eyes flickered open and he squeezed out the words.

"The shame! I'm killed by the shame of what you've become!"

The wailing daughter begged for forgiveness from her father explaining,

"Father, forgive me! I only wanted nice things...for me and for the family. I wanted to send money to you and the only way I could find to do it was by becoming a prostitute."

The old man opened his eyes wide, sat up in the bed and hugged his bereft daughter saying,

"Prostitute? I thought you said Protestant!"

THE FRIARS

A brotherhood of Catholic friars was behind in their rent on their monastery. The head friar came up with the idea that they could make some money by selling flowers from their huge church garden in town.

Two of the friars were chosen to set up a small florist stand at the town market. The public responded favorably and soon a lot of flowers were being sold at a nice profit for the monastery payment.

But, a small florist on the other side of town wasn't happy about the new development. His sales were going down.

He decided to visit the two friars at their stand and explain his predicament. The friars listened patiently to the small man but, in the end, told him that the welfare of monastery was more important than his petty complaints, and that they intended to stay open.

This enraged the little man who stormed out and went immediately to his brother-in-law's house. His sister's husband, Hugh La-Bron, was a vicious ape of a man who was known far and wide for his explosive temper and mean vengefulness.

Feigning tears in his eyes, the small florist told his brother-in-law that the two friars had insulted and disrespected him and in so doing were disrespecting his sister and also Hugh himself!

Hugh's tiny pig-like eyes squinted open. The rage boiled. His huge ham-like arm smashed down on the table, and in a huff, he disappeared out the door headed in the direction of the friars stand.

The next day, the two badly beaten friars returned home to the monastery - never to open their business again.

Thus proving that,

"Hugh, and only Hugh can prevent florist friars!"

DONATIONS

The parish priest answers the phone one day.

"Hello, is this the 'Lady of Grace Church'?"

"Yes it is."

"Yes, I'm calling from the Internal Revenue Service. We were wondering if you could give us a little assistance?"

"I can."

"Wonderful! Do you know a Ryan Newby?"

"Yes I do."

"Is he a regular member of your church?"

"He is."

"Did he donate $20,000? to your church?"

"He will."

******

    The same Catholic priest was assigned to a new parish out in the rural countryside.

    One day, an old widower appeared at the church door carrying the carcass of a dog in his arms. The wizened old man explained that his pet dog had died and because the animal had been such a faithful companion over the years, he was wondering if a Mass could be said for the his poor pet

    The priest replied that he couldn't say services for a strange animal in his church but that there was a Methodist church down the road that might be able to help him.

    The sad little man replied,

"Thank you Father. Do you think $1000. will be enough of a donation for them to do the service?"

    The priest grabbed the dead creature's paws and quickly arranged them together to form a cross, then exclaimed,

    "My God man, why didn't you tell me the poor dog was a Catholic!"

CONVERSION

A new neighbor Ed, who lived in a mostly Catholic Boston neighborhood, had recently converted to Roman Catholicism. His happy Catholic neighbors surrounded him and chanted,

"Born a Protestant.
 Raised a Protestant.
 But now you are a Catholic."

The following month was the celebration of Easter. On the Good Friday before Easter the entire neighborhood was dutifully fasting in anticipation of the celebration of the resurrection. All, except Ed.

Ed's next-door neighbors watched with horror as he placed big slabs of beef spare ribs on his backyard barbeque.

The priest was called to intervene and speak to Ed about the rules of fasting. Ed seemed unconcerned as the priest arrived and explained the restrictions on the eating of meat. Instead, Ed heaped another big spoonful of sauce onto the ribs and chanted over them,

"Born a cow.
 Raised a cow.
 But now you are a fish."

EPITAPHS

Two great spiritual leaders were at a funeral for a respected statesman. Staring into the dear departed's coffin, the first man asked the second how he would wish to be remembered and what words he would like to hear his followers say over his own casket? The man thought for a second and stoking the whiskers of his long white beard replied,

"THAT I WAS A WONDERFUL TEACHER AND SERVANT OF GOD WHO TOUCHED THE LIVES OF MANY."

And what would you like your followers to say?

The second smiled blissfully and replied that he'd like to hear them say,

"LOOK, HE'S MOVING!"

THE SHAMAN

The Indian chief was suffering from a truly terrible stomachache that wouldn't go away. Seeking out the tribe's shaman (medicine man), he asked for help with it.

The shaman listened to the chief's symptoms and then went into a brief trance. Waking from a vision, he tells the chief that to be cured, he must take a small bite out of the tribe's sacred leather thong. This thong had been worn by a great tribal warrior of the past and was much revered as a vessel of the brave's courage and strength.

The chief took the shriveled leather pouch back to his teepee with him. The thought of where the thong had rested and the ancient stains on it caused the chief some unease.

But as a new spasm rocked his stomach, the chief did as he had been instructed and placed his teeth on the ancient garment and bit off a small piece, which he dutifully swallowed with a grimace.

This practice continued for the next two weeks.

At the end of which, the chief sought out the shaman again.
The shaman asked whether the chief now felt any better.
To which the chief replied,

"No, the thong is gone, but the malady lingers on!"

ANGEL WISHES

God's Angels had noticed that a particular minister had been especially devoted and had helped many people. One Sunday they decided to reward the man while he still lived and appeared at his Sunday service. In front of his entire congregation, they praised his good works and offered him a special reward.

He would be given his choice of any one of three gifts. A billion dollars, the good looks of a movie star or the IQ of a genius.

The man thought for a second and since he felt he was already decent looking and had a sense of prosperity about life, he would chose to be a genius.

The Angels acknowledged his choice and disappeared in a flurry of wings.

The minister was left standing there in all of his divine wisdom and genius intelligence.

One of his church members finally asked him to say something to them from his new 'knowing'.

Looking around at his flock, the minister could only say,

"I SHOULD HAVE TAKEN THE MONEY!"

THE CAT

A pious church-going woman looked out her back window with horror. Her beloved collie had the neighbor's cat in its jaws and was savagely shaking the poor creature back and forth. By the time the woman rushed into the yard to extricate the poor creature, its limp disheveled body was just a mass of dirty torn tissue.

She took the cat into her house and washed it gently in her bathtub. The cat was cleaner but no life remained. The poor woman didn't know what to do.

Finally she decided to comb the cat's fur and cover up the worst of the wounds. When she finished, the cat looked peacefully asleep. That night the woman took the cat back to it's own yard and propped it up in the little cat bed on the neighbor's outside porch. With that, the woman snuck back to her own house.

The next morning she cringed as blood-curdling shrieks came from the neighbor's yard. She got up and walked over to the neighbor's fence to innocently ask what was wrong.

Her still shrieking neighbor could barely reply,

"Our cat! Our cat! He died last week and we buried him. And now he's come back!"

TIME MACHINE

A priest, who was also a scientist, had some questions about his faith and to get the answers, he invented a time machine. Using it, he went back in time to the very first Easter Sunday and located the unresurrected body of Jesus Christ.

The priest arrived just in time to see Jesus rising from

the dead and the priest's faith was renewed.

Concerned for his parishioners and their faith as well, he had remembered to take along a camera to bring back pictures for them. Blushingly, he asked the newly-risen Christ if he would mind a few pictures.

Jesus consented willingly and even posed for several shots. The priest thanked him and got back into the time machine. Upon his return, the priest tried to have the pictures developed but they were all blank.

The priest mournfully checked his camera and found that its batteries were drained. Thus he proved the old adage,

"THE SPIRIT IS WILLING BUT THE FLASH IS WEAK."

THE PARROT

An older minister received a big package from his missionary son in Africa. Inside was a beautifully colored parrot with a note wishing the father a happy birthday. The minister was thrilled with the gift until he tried to get the parrot to speak.

From the parrot's mouth came a string of profanity and cussing that turned the air blue! Doing his best to quiet the outrageous bird, he wondered what to do. First he tried prayer, but the bird's language only seemed to get worst. Then he tried patience and gently spoke only loving words to the bird for over a month.

At the end of the month he cautiously offered the parrot a cracker. Again, he was met with loud expletives. Just then, he heard a female member of the church board at their door being greeted by his wife. The minister panicked and threw the still-cussing bird into the refrigerator.

After the lady board member left, he retrieved the parrot. The shivering bird stepped out onto his extended arm and spoke,

"I wish to extend my apology for my crude language..."

The minister was pleased and a bit taken aback by the quick change. Then the bird continued,

"And what, may I ask, was it that the CHICKEN in there said?"

THE PEARLY GATES

A famous evangelist died and appeared at the gates to Heaven. The Angel stationed at the gate asked the man what he wanted.

"I want to enter Heaven."

"And what have you done in your life that makes you feel you belong here?"

The evangelist thought for a while and answered,

"Besides preaching to the masses, I once saw a bum on the street and gave him 50 cents."

"Anything else?'

"Yeah sure, I also gave 50 cents to a hungry little boy."

"Anything Else?'

"Nope."

The Angel turned to the golden phone located next to the gate and spoke with Saint Peter. The Angel reviewed the encounter over the phone and asked what they should do with this evangelist.
Saint Peter's answer was to,

"GIVE HIM HIS DOLLAR BACK AND TELL HIM TO GO TO HELL."

FORGIVENESS

In the middle of the sermon on Easter Sunday, the minister asked all those in the congregation who were willing to forgive their enemies, to raise their hands. All the hands of the members reached skyward – with the noticeable exception of Mrs. Grimace.

Mrs. Grimace was an elderly widow seated in the very front row. The minister walked down to Mrs. Grimace and asked her,
"Are you not ready to forgive your enemies?"

"Sure I am. But, I don't have any."

"How old are you Mrs. Grimace?"

"Eighty-nine."

"Eighty-nine and not an enemy in the world! Please step up to the podium Mrs. Grimace and share with us some of your secrets of living such a full life and not having any enemies."

Mrs. Grimace pulled her aged body up to the podium and leaning into the microphone, explained loudly,

"It's really no big secret . . . I just outlived the rotten bitches."

THE QUIZ

Two young ministers, fresh from seminary school, were both interested in the same newly-open position at a large city ministry. The church board looked closely at the qualifications of the two young men and found them closely matched in almost every way.

Both were asked to deliver a Sunday sermon and both did so eloquently. Afterwards, the church members were surveyed and it was obvious that the congregation was evenly split between the two men.

The senior member of the church board was asked to prepare a quiz to test the Bible knowledge of the two candidates. The winning candidate would be chosen from their answers to this all-important quiz.

The church elder took his task seriously and prepared ten questions arranged in an increasing order of difficulty. He would also be grading the quiz and delivering the results to the board.

The test began with both candidates writing furiously and with great intensity. When the allotted time ran out the church elder collected both exams. An hour later he returned the graded exams to each man. As might be expected, they had both answered nine of the ten questions correctly.

That night the church board called the men back in and awarded the ministerial position to the first of the two men with condolences to the second. The second candidate was filled with indignation and demanded an explanation from the board.

Quietly, the church elder, who had prepared the quiz, took the young man aside. He explained that the appointment had been made not on the answers that had been given, but rather based on the one incorrect answer. The man still did not understand until the elder held the two answers up for him to compare.

The winning candidate had written,

"I don't know." to the final question.

The loser had written,

"Neither do I".

Section Two

Little Bits and Pieces

In this section we will be sharing some short jokes, anecdotes, fun lists and one-liners.

Enjoy!

Joy is felt anew when shared.

The Chicken

A man confesses to a priest in the church confessional that he has stolen his neighbor's chicken. The priest is about to give him a stiff penance for his sin, but the man interrupts and says,
"But I didn't harm the chicken in any way and ... it was just a joke."

The priest asks the man how far he had taken the stolen chicken. When the man replied "three miles', the priest gave him a stiff penance anyway for, as he explained later,
"Taking a joke too far."

Marriage

My wife and I were happy for over twenty years - then we got married.

The secret of a good marriage remains a secret.

The minister's wife suspected he was involved with his church secretary. The lipstick stains on his collar had been covered with whiteout.

A good wife always forgives her husband when she's wrong.

What men want in marriage? To find someone to be very, very, very close to ...... who will leave them alone.

Asked why she wore her wedding ring on the wrong finger, she replied, "I married the wrong man."

The minister said he had not spoken to his wife in over a month - he didn't want to interrupt her.

I married Miss Right but, I didn't know her first name was, 'Always".

My girlfriend said we couldn't even talk about sex until we were married. On our honeymoon she said,
'Okay, now we can talk about it."

My wife told me I should be more affectionate - so I got a girlfriend.

Losing a wife can be very hard - but for me it's been darn near impossible.

The church has developed a very profitable program providing marriage counseling in the community.
It successfully combines the two things that most women like to do best ... talk and spend money.

It can be helpful to talk to your wife as much as possible while you are making love.... provided that a phone is handy.

A husband told his wife that men are like fine wines that improve with age.... So she locked him in the cellar.

The minister advised the young wife to take more of an interest in her husband's activities. She did.... she hired a detective.

False Teeth

An older Lutheran minister was seated next to a layperson at a large ecumenical conference. He confided to the stranger,

"I am scheduled to be the next speaker but I left my false teeth behind in my hotel room."

The man smiled back and said,

"Reverend, God must be listening to your prayers because I happen to have an extra pair of false teeth in my briefcase."

In amazement and deep gratitude the minister took the proffered teeth from the man and inserted them in his mouth. They were too wide.

"Here said the man, I have another set that might fit you better."

The minister tried this set, but they were too small.

The man took a third set out of his case and assured the minister that this set would be the right one.

The minister inserted the teeth into his mouth and indeed, they were a perfect fit! Gratefully he shook the man's hand and praising God; he thanked his providence for seating him next to a dentist.

To which the stranger replied,

"No, not a dentist. Just an undertaker."

Temple of Boris Blatt

A young Buddhist from China opened a temple in the western part of the United States and named it 'Boris Blatt's Temple of Buddhist Unity'.

A visitor to the temple admired the simple beauty and purity of its construction. But when he met the young Buddhist, he couldn't help asking about the temple's strange name - who was Boris Blatt?

The young Buddhist priest explained in very broken English that when he had immigrated to the United States, the man in front of him in the immigration line had been named Boris Blatt.

And, when the immigration official had asked the young Buddhist his name, He had replied proudly,

"Sam Ting".

Hen Pecked

At the gates of Heaven, St. Peter was speaking to a group of recently arrived male souls.

"All of you men who were the bosses in your homes while on Earth please step to the right."

"All of you men who were subservient to your wives step to your left.

A line quickly formed on the left leaving only one frail looking little man standing by himself to the right.

St. Peter looked ominously at the small man and asked,

"What makes you feel you should be on that side?'

The man replied in a timid voice,

"Because that's where my wife told me to stand ."

Divine Cradle

One night after recently giving birth, a young minister's wife observed her husband standing over the baby's crib. On his face she observed the mixed emotions of awe, wonder, amazement and humility.

With love in her eyes, she joined her husband, put her arm around him and asked gently what thoughts were in his mind?

"It is truly amazing," he relied softly,
"How could anyone make a crib of this quality for only $49.99 and still make a profit?"

Go - Getter

There was a young priest who was well-known for his ambition and desire to move ahead in the Catholic hierarchy. When the young man heard that the local bishop had been in the hospital and wasn't expected to recover, he raced to the cardinal's office and asked for an audience with his superior.

When the cardinal bade him enter, the young priest didn't even wait to sit down before blurting,

"I've heard that the bishop may be leaving us, bless his soul. I want you to know that I am interested in taking his place."

The cardinal looked at the young priest, scratched his chin and nodded to himself as he answered,

"Don't you think we should check with the undertaker first?"

Two Sweaters

A Jewish Rabbi received two sweaters from his mother - in-law to celebrate the New Year. When she next came to visit them, he wore one of the sweaters.
Looking at him in the sweater, her only comment was,

"Didn't you like the other one?"

Grass

The Pope was riding through the countryside in his limousine when he saw all these poor people on their knees eating grass by the roadside. He ordered his driver to stop and getting out, asked the peasants why they were eating the grass?

"Because we don't have enough money for food."

The Pope shook his head and motioned for the poor villagers to crowd into his limousine with him.

"Come along with me then. I'll take care of you. I know where there's some grass on the Vatican lawn that's at least six inches taller."

Irish Memories

An Irish priest goes into the neighborhood bar after imbibing on a bit too much of the sacrificial wine. He is just sitting down and getting comfortable when one of the men at the bar jumps up grabs him by the shoulder and yells,

"Patty, Patty. Get up. Your house is on fire."

The priest gets up, runs to the door, then stops and thinks,

"Hey. I 'm a priest. I live in the church. I don't have a house."

The priest returns to his seat at the rear of the bar and is settling in as another man jumps up excitedly and yells for him to follow,

"Patty, Patty, hurry and come with me. Your wife is dying!"

The priest runs to the door before realizing,

"Hey. I'm a priest. I don't have a wife."

Back at his table the priest is putting his feet up and getting ready for a little nap when he is shaken awake.

"Patty, Patty get up. You've just won the Irish sweepstakes! Let's get to the telegraph office and collect your money."

The priest jumps up and rushes out the door. Running down the street he realizes,

"Hey. My names not Patty."

New Mercedes

A man had just purchased his first Mercedes Benz and was so proud of it that he invited a priest, a minister and a rabbi to come by and bless the vehicle for him.

The priest sprinkled it with holy water and chanted a prayer in Latin.

The minister invoked the name of Jesus Christ and led them all in silent prayer.

The Rabbi sang a psalm and then cut off the end of the ~~tailpipe.~~ exhaust.

New Nuns

There was some concern amongst the staff at the church convent that the newest sisters were not very bright. After a swimming competition, one of the new sisters had come in last in the hundred-meter breaststroke. Afterwards she had complained to the Mother Superior that she had seen the others sisters cheating.

"How so," asked the Mother Superior?

"I saw them using their arms."

****

The same nun was seen returning a new scarf at the department store after Christmas. When asked if she didn't like the color, she replied,
"The color was fine. It was just too tight on me."

****

The new nun, when told that a case of syphilis had been discovered in the convent replied,

"Good. I was getting tired of the Chablis."

Heard by our Spiritual Counselor

"Reverend, my husband thinks he is a refrigerator."

"That is a little odd. But does he treat you with respect and honor your spiritual vows?"

"Yes, that part is fine. But when he sleeps with his mouth open, that little light keeps coming on."

****

"I used to dream all the time that I had lived a past life as a Russian wolfhound. It kept me from sleeping properly so, I finally went to a psychiatrist to figure it out."

"How do you feel now."?

"Great! Just feel my nose."

****

"I had a lengthy operation for gallstones. The operation was successful but I think the surgeon may have left a sponge or something inside of me."

"Why do you think that? Are you having pains?"

"No. But boy do I get thirsty."

"I got my wife a lovely ladies wristwatch for her birthday. But she still won't speak to me."

"Didn't she like it?'

"Yes. But the lady came and took it back."

****

A man walks into the minister's office for spiritual counseling. He has a carrot up his nose, a green bean in his left ear and some celery in his right ear. He looks at the minister and asks,

"Reverend, I don't seem to have any energy lately. I don't have any interest in my wife and I don't even want to get up to go to work in the morning. What's wrong with me?"

"You're not eating properly."

The Carpenter and the Cabinetmakers

Many Christian historians find it odd that Jesus, who was a carpenter, chose so many fishermen instead of something more closely related like - cabinetmakers - to be his apostles. That was, until it was explained to them that Jesus would have been loathe to say,

"Drop your drawers and follow me".

Blind Monks

A young nun was alone at the convent on a Saturday afternoon. She decided to take a bath and had just finished disrobing when there was a knock at the front door.

"Who is it?'

"The Blind Monk."

The young woman gets a little thrill as she realizes he can't see her and lets the man in while she is still standing there naked. As she searches for something to give the poor man, he asks.

"And where would you like me to hang your new blinds, Sister?"

Blind and Mute Monks

What did the blind monk do as he fell down the stairway?
- He screamed his fingers off.
How did the blind monk burn the side of his face?
- He answered the iron by mistake.
How did the blind monk burn the other side of his face?
-They called back.
Why didn't the blind monk scream falling down the stairs again?
- He was wearing mittens.
What did the blind monk consider 'light' reading?
- The stucco wall in his room.
What is the blind monk's favorite color?
- Corduroy.
The monastery was burglarized while the blind monk was in charge. He would have done more to help but the fiendish robbers held his hands so he couldn't yell for help.

Got Milk

There was an old nun at the church convent that had taught there for many years. Her body was now infirm and it was painful for her to get up in the morning. The Mother Superior called for a doctor to see the poor woman.

The doctor saw the nun and in private told the Mother Superior that the woman was terminally ill and the best thing to do to ease her pain would be to give her a shot of whiskey three times a day.

The Mother Superior tried to give the nun a drink of whiskey but the nun refused saying she had lived too long with God to now be tempted by worldly pleasures.

The Mother Superior tried another plan. She knew the old nun loved to drink milk so, she ordered the kitchen staff to mix the whiskey with the nun's milk each day. The old nun drank the milk without complaint and it seemed to ease her suffering.

By the end of the year the old nun was fading fast and all the sisters gathered around her. The Mother Superior asked the old nun if there was any important advice or spiritual truths that the old nun had learned over the years that she could share with the younger nuns.

"Only one," she croaked. "Whatever you do, never sell that cow."

Camping

Two friars named Brother Alphonse and Brother Dominic went out camping in the forest behind the monastery. They found a nice level spot in a field near a creek and set up their tent.

After a wonderful supper by the campfire, they put out the fire and climbed into their sleeping bags to meditate and go to sleep. Several hours went by and then Brother Dominic nudged Brother Alphonse and asked him to look up at the sky.

Alphonse's eyes gazed upward. The stars shone brightly in a celestial ballet above them. He heard himself describing aloud the beauty above them,

"God is all powerful. We are small and weak in comparison. His majesty shineth on us beyond all understanding. I lie here in awe and wonder."

To which Brother Dominic replied,

"No. Not that you dummy! Somebody stole our tent."

Almonds

A bus full of elderly nuns is on its way to the Vatican. One of the nuns taps the bus driver on the shoulder and offers him a handful of almonds. The hungry driver gratefully takes them and munches on them as they continue down the highway.

A little later, the same nun taps the shoulder of the driver and offers him some more almonds. He takes them, snacks on them, and this continues several times until they finally reach the Vatican.

As the nuns gather their things to get off the bus, the curious driver asks the elderly nun why the sisters were so generous and why they didn't eat some of the almonds themselves -weren't they hungry?

The little Nun smiled and explained that with their old teeth, they were unable to eat almonds.

The driver was still puzzled and asked,

"If you can't eat the almonds, why do you buy them instead of something else?'

The little nun smiled naughtily and replied,

"We just like to suck the chocolate off of them!"

The Three Wise Men

A man from Massachusetts was visiting friends in a small southern town in Georgia. It was almost Christmas and the town's people had erected a beautiful nativity scene in front of the town hall.

The depiction of Joseph and Mary and baby Jesus in the manger brought back pleasant memories. It would have been a perfect memory of his youth except for the fireman's helmets worn by the three Magi.

He asked his friend about the helmets. Weren't they able to find more suitable headgear for the three wise men?

His friend just laughed and replied,

"Don't you Yankees ever read your bibles?'

He assured her that they did indeed read their bibles. But to the best of his memory, there was no mention of firemen at Jesus' birth.

His friend just happened to have her bible in her backpack and took it out. She thumbed to the relevant page and pointed out the appropriate passage for him.

He looked at the page in wonder and read,

"Three wise men came from AFAR."

Truly Needy

After the Sunday worship service a young boy stopped on the way out of church to talk to the new minister.

"When I grow up and have a job, I'm going to come by the church every week and give you all my money."

"Well thank you young man. And just what inspired you to think of such a generous act?"

"Because," said the earnest little boy, "my father said you were one of the poorest ministers we have ever had."

Jewish Quickies

Why did the Jewish moyl retire?

-He just couldn't cut it anymore.

Do Jewish women use facial cream?

-Yes. It's called oil of 'oy vey'

How do you insult a Jewish mother?

-Tell people she pays retail.

In the Jewish faith, when does a fetus become a human being?

-When he graduates from medical school.

If Tarzan and Jane were Jewish what would cheetah be?

-A fur coat.

What did the Jewish mother say to her daughter when informed that she had been having an affair?

-Who catered it?

Why do Jewish mothers bottle-feed their babies instead of breast-feeding them?

-It hurts too much to boil the nipples.

What kind of cigarettes do Jewish rabbis prefer?

-Gefiltered.

Reality Check

How do you know if something really exists or if it is just an illusion?

Kick it really hard.

Adam & Eve

The Sunday School teacher asked her students to draw a picture of their favorite story from the Bible. At the end of the first hour the children handed in their drawings. The teacher commented on each one, praising each child for either their wonderful blue color in 'Jonah & the Whale' or the realistic figures in Jesus' feeding of the multitudes in the 'Loaves and the Fishes'.

Little Sammy was the last in line to turn in his picture. The teacher hoped to find something positive to say to Sammy because he had been struggling to keep up with the other kids in the class. But, as she looked at his picture she was speechless.

In Sammy's picture two very naked people were rolling around in the backseat of a large car driven by a bearded hippie. Flipping the picture over to hide it from the other children, she tried to contain her upset as she asked,

"Sammy. What is this?"

"Gee teacher," replied Sammy, "it's a Cadillac."

"No Sammy. I mean what Bible story is this supposed to represent?'

"Don't you remember teacher? It's just like you said - God driving Adam and Eve out of Heaven."

Meditation

Two Rabbis were walking down the street. One stops and asks the other how he is doing. He answers,

"Fine, and how are you?"

"I'm good, thanks."

"And how is your family? Is your eldest son still unemployed?"

"Yes, he hasn't been able to find anything just yet. But he is meditating a lot in the meantime."

"Meditating, what's that?"

"I'm not certain - but it sure beats sitting around doing nothing!"

More Meditation

Four monks were practicing meditation at the Tibetan monastery. Suddenly, the prayer flag at the top of the building unfurled and started rippling ferociously in the gust of wind.
    The newest monk looked up from his meditation and said, "The prayer flag is flapping."
    The monk next to him looked up and corrected the first, "No, it is the wind that is flapping."
    The third monk hearing this looked up and stated, " Both wrong. Mind is flapping."
    The fourth monk, who was also the eldest, continued to meditate with head bowed. But not before whispering,

 "All wrong.... It is mouths that are flapping."

To Change a Light Bulb

Catholics – none. They prefer candles.

Muslims - none. Allah has predestined when the lights will go on and off.

Evangelicals - one, and easily, because their hands are up in the air already.

Native American shamans - five. One to change the bulb and four to sing the 'light bulb changing song'.

Mormons - Eight. One man to change the bulb and seven wives to tell him how to do it.

Jehovah witnesses - fifty. One to change it and forty-nine to pray against the forces of the dark.

Druids - one hundred. One to change the bulb and ninety-nine to move the stones.

Baptists - Changgggge?????

New age - none. They prefer to charge up their crystals and watch them glow.

Course in Miracles students - sorry, we don't know. That material is copyrighted.

Amish - 'what's a light bulb?'

Youth ministers - ? They aren't around long enough.

Atheists - one, but they are still in darkness.

Zen Buddhists - one to change it, one not to change it.

Gurus - the universe changes it, we get the heck out of the way.

Mormons - how many will fit in the room?

Surgeons in your congregation - why don't you let us remove the socket entirely? You're not using it anyway and it'll just cause you problems in the future.

How many years will it take twenty gay priests to change it?
It depends on how long it takes to get one out of the closet?

Celibacy

It was reported that a new pill was recently discovered that was guaranteed to cure celibacy.
But.... the Catholic Church found it too hard to swallow!

Nuns

When the price of sugar recently doubled, the upset nuns began to raise cane.

Did you hear about the nun that got pregnant - they investigated and found out she liked to dress as an altar boy.

Five novitiate Catholic nuns were about to take their final vows when the ceremony was interrupted by the late arrival of three unknown Jewish rabbis. The late guests were asked where they would like to be seated and they answered,
"On the groom's side."

Texan in Paris

A Baptist minister from Texas was visiting Paris with his wife for the first time. His brother-in-law Pierre had been born in France and was serving as a tour guide for the couple. As they went by the Eiffel Tower Pierre pointed it out and explained how it had been constructed in less than two years.

"Shoot," said the Texas minister, "a little old tower like that we could put up in under two weeks in Texas."

Next they drove by Notre Dame Cathedral and Pierre described how it had taken hundreds of years to finally finish the construction, but that it was now the largest cathedral in Europe.

"Shucks said the Texan. We could build something like that in under a year in Texas."

Pierre was now visibly getting a little upset with his boorish visitor. But saying nothing he continued their tour out into the countryside. Coming to the top of a small hill the sprawling majesty of the palatial homes of King Louis and Napoleon at Versailles came into view.

"Wowww!" said the Texas minister, "What's that over there?'

Pierre replied with a smile,

"Damned if I know. Wasn't there yesterday."

Viagra

The Pope recently ordered a Vatican plane to fly over Notre Dame cathedral spraying viagra. He wanted to straighten out all the hunchbacks.

When the plane got back there was still some viagra left over so, they sent it over to the Vatican rest home for retired priests. It's given to the older priests at nighttime to keep them from rolling out of bed.

Confession

An elderly Catholic gentleman who lived in Holland went to a local church for confession after a fifty-year absence. He walked into the confessional and confided to the priest there.

"Father, forgive me for my sins. It has been over fifty years since my last confession. I have lived a good life but I wish to confess that during World War II a beautiful young Jewish girl came to my door and asked me to hide her from the Germans. She was not a Catholic but I let her in and hid her in my attic."

The priest responded, "Even though the girl was not of our faith, it was a Christian responsibility to help her and you committed no sin in taking her in."

"No," said the old man. "It was much worse than that Father. I allowed the young girl to repay me with sexual favors."

The priest recoiled a bit before saying,

"What you did then was a sin but, I can understand that under the circumstances ... being under the same roof together ... that these things happen. So now, if you are truly sorry for what happened, you will be forgiven."

The old man sighed with relief and then continued,

"One more thing Father?"

"Yes?" said the priest.

"Should I tell her the war is over?"

Jewish Mothers

A young rabbi was about to be married. He goes home to tell his mother and decides to test her intuition by introducing her to three different woman he has dated and letting her guess which one will be his new bride.

Each of the women has different attributes. One is tall and dark-haired. The second is short, thin and blonde. The third is overweight with flaming red-hair.

His Jewish mother accepts his challenge and with a quick scan of the three women announces,

"She's the thin blonde."

The young rabbi was amazed that his mother had correctly identified his fiancée.

"But Mama, how did you know? You haven't met any of these girls before - have you?

"No. But it was easy. I could tell right away. I already can't stand the blonde."

The Heavenly 'Baker'

Genesis - in the beginning there were no cookies.

Adam & Eve - took a bite out of the first cookies.

Noah - liked two chocolate chip, two mallomars, two
        oreos, two sugar cookies .....

Moses - commanded the cookies to 'part'.

Atheists - there is no cookie baker.

Evolutionists - the cookies make themselves.

Buddhists - to die with no cookies.

Hinduism - no beef on my cookies please.

Confucianism - if the cookie gets wet, it is no longer dry.

Muslim - he, who breaks the most infidel cookies, wins.

Judaism - he who follows the recipe wins.

Mormons - boys can have as many cookies as they want.

Jehovah's witness - sell their cookies door to door.

Calvinists - you must earn your cookies.

Christian science - keep your cookies healthy.

Course in Miracles - you are the cookie you love.

Seventh day Adventists - like their cookies best on Saturdays.

Baptists - prefer their cookies dipped in water.

Catholics - he who denies himself the most cookies, wins.

Stoicism - I broke my cookie, but I can handle it.

Communism - share your cookies.

Polytheism - there are many bakers.

Capitalism - more cookies please.

Rastafarianism - I prefer to smoke my cookies.

Frisbeetarianism - when you die, your cookie gets stuck up on the roof.

HMO's

Every time I hear the Christmas story about Mary and Joseph having to deliver the baby Jesus in a manger, I have to wonder whether they had the same medical plan that I do.

The Bishop's Library

The bishop purchased two new books for the church library. The first was a book 'How to Deal with Hair Loss'. The bishop decided not to keep it because the pages KEPT FALLING OUT.

The other book was 'Dealing with Impotence as we Age'. The bishop tried to put it in the library bookcase but had to get rid of it because he COULDN'T GET IT TO STAND UP.

Disposition

The priest was counseling a newly married woman from his parish. She seemed very irritable and avoided any responses to his questions about any problems in her marital relationship. Finally he asked,

"Did you wake up grumpy this morning?"

Her response.

"No. I just let him sleep in."

Favorite Sermon

"The Bible tells us that 'blessed are the merciful'.
This sermon is now over."

****

George Burns once explained that the secret of a good sermon is to have a good beginning and a good ending.... and to have the two as close together as possible!

****

On a beautiful Sunday morning the wise old minister addressed the congregation and announced that he had prepared three different sermons. A $1000 sermon that lasts five minutes, a $500 sermon that lasts thirty minutes and a $100 sermon that lasts an hour.

"We will now take up a collection to decide which one gets delivered today."

****

After the sermon, only one man applauded. He was slapping his head to keep himself awake.

****

After the service, the entire irreverent congregation was hissing except for one man. And he was applauding the hissing.

New Suit

A recently ordained minister was proudly ordering a new suit from the town tailor. After the measurements the minister whispered to the tailor that he was sorry, but he wouldn't have the funds to pay for the new suit for another six months.

The tailor, who was part of the man's new congregation, whispered back that it was all right with him.

Relieved, the minister asked him when his new suit would be ready?

To which the tailor replied,
"Oh, about six months."

Fiery Sermons

The Pentecostal minister had been gradually losing membership in his church. Not being able to figure out why, he took a folio of his most recent sermons to the most senior minister in the region and asked if he should be putting more fire into his sermons.

The older (and wiser) man looked through the sermons and offered just these words of advice,

"No. I think you should be doing just the opposite."

Words of Wisdom

God provides food for the mouths of every bird.
But he does not just throw it into their nests.

PMS

After a long Sunday sermon describing how the bible speaks to every condition in the human experience, the older minister was asked by one of the ladies in private.

"What about PMS? Does the bible say anything about Pre - Menstrual Syndrome?"

The minister replied confidently that though no verse came to him at that moment, he was sure that he could find a bible reference about PMS and would share it with her the following week.

The minister looked diligently through his bible line by line that week and when the woman approached him the following Sunday, he pointed out a particular verse to her and read aloud,

"And Mary rode Joseph's ass all the way to Bethlehem."

Gandhi

Mahatmas Gandhi was once asked during a visit to the English parliament in London, what he thought of western civilization?
To which he replied, "I think it would be a good idea."

Location, Location, Location

Reverend Beasley had the new church built on a large lot with a nice view but.... he failed to notice that they were building it next to a fire hydrant factory. And that the on -street parking was.... how shall we say it? ... Very limited.

Thanksgiving

The Indian shaman knew his people were in trouble at that first Thanksgiving when the Pilgrims started to sing, " This land was your land, this land is my land."

Last Thanksgiving, I decided to go out and shoot my own turkey. It was fun. But, now they won't let me back into the grocery store.

If you want something a little different for Thanksgiving dinner this year, try swan. They roast well and hold a lot more stuffing.

This year we decided to celebrate Thanksgiving in a more 'traditional way'. We invited everyone in the neighborhood to our house for an enormous home-cooked feast... then afterwards, we killed them and took their land.

Mark Twain

It is said that while Mark Twain was in England speaking to a literary society gathering, he was asked whether he believed that Shakespeare himself had written his plays or had it been someone else?
At first he replied that he had not given it much thought.
But one of the members pressed him for an opinion and he answered,

"I think I'll wait until I get to Heaven and then just ask Shakespeare himself who wrote the plays."

The Englishman who had pressed for the opinion was not satisfied with this response and shouted back,

"Mr. Twain, I don't believe you will find Mr. Shakespeare in Heaven.'

To which Twain replied,

"Then you ask him."

Face Down

The angry minister warned a young rebellious punk that if he didn't straighten out his life, that he, the minister, would see to it that he would be buried face down at the end of his li fe.

The punk just replied with a sneer,

"Why's that?"

The minister glowered right back and said,

"So that you can SEE where you are going."

Signals that your Neighbor may be a Muslim

He thinks that the costumes on 'Pioneer House' and 'Little House on the Prairie' are way too provocative.

He uses the backyard barbeque in the winter.

His wife brings you homemade shawarma.

He thinks 'Pepsi' begins with a 'b'.

While gardening, he always kneels facing Mecca.

That abnormally large dog of his has a long blunt nose and two humps.

He offers you a barbequed quail leg that looks suspiciously like squirrel.

Haircuts

A young monk was giving some of the older monks haircuts. His wrist slipped and he nicked an older monk's ear causing it to bleed. Apologetically, he begged for forgiveness and then asked the older monk if he could wrap his head in a warm towel.

"No," hissed the distressed older monk,
"I think I'll just take it home under my arm."

Baby Names

The crotchety old Greek farmer had finally fathered his first child with a much younger wife. The Orthodox priest asked at the baby's baptism what name they had given the child. The old farmer looked at the tiny wrinkled up baby held by his wife and said,

"Theophilus."

"Ahh, that's an interesting name. How did you come to chose it?"

"Because," said the farmer, "it's the -oplil-us looking baby I've ever seen."

Trust Me

A neurotic young man went to his minister for counseling and shared his main issue.

"Reverend, I have this terrible feeling that everyone's always trying to take advantage of me."

The minister tells him to relax. These feelings he has been having are perfectly normal. Everyone thinks like that once in a while and he has nothing to worry about.

The young man breathes a sigh of relief. Gratefully he gets up to leave and asks how much he should donate to the church for this session.

The minister replies,

"HOW MUCH HAVE YOU GOT?"

Graffiti

A new addition to the church school was being built. The senior minister looked out his window to observe the project. Shocked, he sees several of the Sunday School children pressing their hands and names into the newly poured concrete.

Dashing out of his office, he screams loudly and shakes his fist at the offenders as they scampered away.

One of the ladies of the congregation witnessed the outburst and asked the minister,

"Reverend, aren't men of God supposed to love little children?"

To which he agitatedly replied,

"Yes, in the abstract. But not in the concrete."

Bathrooms

An American minister was visiting Spain. He had to use the bathroom desperately but couldn't remember the Spanish word for bathroom. And, the last we heard, he was still rushing down the road asking directions to the 'Juan'.

Early Christians

The minister was trying to explain to the Sunday School class how difficult were the times in which the Early Christians lived. He explained how the very first Christians had no machines to make their lives easier.

To wash things they had to take them down to the river wrapped in sheets and slam them against the rocks until they were clean.

To which little Reggie replied,

"Wow! That must have been murder on the dishes."

Ten Signs that the New Preacher Might be a Redneck

1. Instead of Reverend, he prefers being called Billy-Bob.

2. Church services always end in time to get home to watch the football game.

3. You have an engine block for a church altar.

4. The last time he mowed his lawn, he found his missing wheelbarrow.

5. He shows up for the Sunday service in cut-offs and a tank top.

6. Instead of a cross above your altar, he has a velvet Elvis.

7. At home, he has to move the weed whacker to take a bath.

8. He performs wedding ceremonies in camouflage gear.

9. He waters his yard by unzipping first.

10. He ends each service with "Y'all come back now Y'hear."

(For redneck priests add - they refill the holy water from a keg.)

TM

A very clumsy fellow who decided to practice transcendental meditation was given the mantra "Oops"

The Yogi

A certain yogi went out and ordered an inexpensive vegetarian meal. Afterwards he thanked the waitress and handed her a twenty-dollar bill. When the girl failed to return to the table, the yogi went looking for her. The perplexed yogi finally found her sitting in the back of the restaurant and asked,

"What happened to my change?"

The waitress smiled, looked up and said,

"Change must come from within."

****

The next night the same yogi went to a Zen pizza parlor. When it was time to order he said,

"Make me one with everything."

****

Back at his ashram, the yogi was asked by a Zen master,

"Why did it take the Buddha so long to vacuum his sofa?"

The yogi meditated for a second before answering correctly,

"Because he didn't have any attachments!"

Answered Prayer

The fire and brimstone minister was in a conciliatory mood after delivering a heated sermon on the 'Dangers of the New Morality'. As an example, he mentioned Brittany Spears, and how she should be more pitied than condemned. He suggested that his church members pray for her.
A young voice from the back of the choir was heard saying,

"I've been praying for her for years. But I never get her."

Fourteen more Hints that your Minister is a Redneck

1. The church candles all have 'Wal-Mart' tags.

2. To get into the church choir, there is a compulsory swimsuit competition.

3. The minister says Adam and Eve were 'nekked'.

4. The handle on the church door is an old deer head.

5. Your church music includes Johnny Cash's 'Ring of Fire' and a chorus of 'Dueling Banjos'.

6. The corners of the church are held up by cinder blocks.

7. The church pews have vinyl seats.

8. The kids in Sunday School watch pay-for-view wrestling to dramatize bible stories.

9. The minister hiccups and his tobacco chaw slips out.

10. The church picnic features a bobbing for French fries in hot oil contest.

11. There is a spittoon on your altar.

12. The communion wine is Mad Dog 20/20.

13. There is a logo of a major farm equipment company on the back of your minister's robe.

14. David slew Goliath. He did not 'kick the crap out of him.'

Good Things About Hell

There is plenty of legal help available for wrongful death lawsuits.

Roomy smoking sections.

It's a 'dry' heat.

The boiling vats of brimstone have been switched to healthier low-fat canola oil.

Watching Satan trying to torture sado-masochists can be very entertaining.

The free daily prostate checks.

The free 'Welcome O.J.' T-shirts.

Stop Signs

Most Catholics coming to a stop sign don't bother to read it but will stop if the car in front of them does.

Most Christian Fundamentalists coming to a stop sign will read it carefully and literally will not go until it tells them to.

Most Orthodox Jews coming to a stop sign immediately turn around and look for another route without a sign so they don't have to risk disobeying it.

Most Reform Jews approach the stop sign contemplating whether it personally applies to them.

Most Mormons don't know when to stop.

Most Muslims are grateful for the sign's reminder to stop and bow to Mecca.

Most Zen Buddhists become 'one' with the stop sign and also with the car that hits them as they meditate.

Viva le Differance

A young Catholic boy was playing in his wading pool with the Protestant daughter of the next-door neighbor. The two kids were having a good time and the little girl suggested that they take their bathing suits off. The little boy's eyes opened wide as the suits came off and he exclaimed,

"Wow, I didn't know there was THAT much of a difference between Catholics and Protestants!"

Spiritualists & Psychics

When two psychics meet on the street, they usually greet each other the same way,

"You are fine, how am I?"

******

One Spiritualist we know refused to hand over the television remote control because, he wanted to 'channel'.

******

Then there was the psychic who was in a car accident.
She had an auto-body experience.

Two psychics were meditating. One said to the other,

"Are you not thinking what I'm not thinking?"

Eating with God

Our favorite restaurant is at an Indian ashram. They have two choices on their entree menu at every meal - take it or leave it.

The same restaurant had bottles of 'Dijon vu' brand mustard at every table. I asked about the new brand. They said it was,

"The same mustard that we'd seen somewhere before."

Vegetarians

Vegetarians sometimes feel that their diet makes them healthier and feel closer to God. But two old vegetarian friends of mine started eating meat again. I asked them why?

"Because we were starting to tilt towards the sun".

These same two friends said that they were also tired of having to call the plumber so often during their vegetarian days. I asked them why their diet would make any difference with their plumbing?
Their answer,

"Because our sink used to have a 'leek' in it."

Then these friends gave up their vegetarian diet for good when their houseplants just started looking 'much too good' to them.

A last word on vegetarians. There is nothing wrong with being a vegetarian. And, some of my best friends are still vegetarians. Of course they are also quadrupeds.

Christian Dating Lines

"I'd like to pray with you."

"Do you believe God has directed us to be together?"

"I know a church where we can go to talk."

"You know Jesus? Me too!"

"God told me to come talk to you."

"Is it a sin that you stole my heart?"

"Nice bible."

"Have you ever tried praying at the drive in movies?"

Say it with Flowers

A young minister in Scotland goes into a flower shop to buy something for his wife on their first anniversary. The shopkeeper shows him a beautiful bouquet of roses for twenty dollars. The minister asks to see something a little less expensive.

The shopkeeper shows the minister a colorful bouquet of mixed flowers for ten dollars. The minister rejects the bouquet and asks the price of a single daisy.

The clerk replies the daisy will only cost one dollar. The minister tells him he'll take the daisy and to please wrap it up. As the clerk is wrapping the lone flower, he asks the minister what it is he is trying to communicate to his wife with this gift?

The reply,

"I am a man of few words."

Spiritual Understanding

"I practice non-attachment"
Really means ... I'm broke and don't have a job.

"I experience oneness and completeness within myself"
Really means ... I don't have any friends.

"That person is just experiencing karma from a past life"
Really means ... Don't expect me to get involved.

"Make us one with everything"
Really means ... don't leave off the mustard, onions or relish.

"I am not this human flesh and blood body"
Really means ... Another dessert please.

"God, I give my life to you"
Really means ... I've tried everything else.

Zen Moments

If you lend someone $20 and never see them again.
-IT WAS PROBABLY WORTH IT. -

If at first you don't succeed.
-SKYDIVING IS NOT FOR YOU. -

Give a man a fish and he will eat for a day. Teach him how to fish and ...
-HE WILL SIT IN A BOAT AND DRINK BEER ALL DAY. -

Your sole purpose in life may be to...
-SERVE AS A WARNING TO OTHERS. -

When testing the depth of the waters...
-DON'T USE BOTH FEET. -

There are two theories about how to reason with women...
-NEITHER OF THEM WORKS. -

Before you criticize someone, you should walk a mile in their shoes.
-THAT WAY IF YOU DO INSULT THEM & THEY GET MAD, YOU'LL BE A MILE AWAY AND STILL HAVE THEIR SHOES.

Ten Signs that you need a New Sunday School Teacher

1. "Teacher, teacher, are you sure this is how they made unleavened bread in the bible?"
- "Shhhh! Just get back in the oven with the other children."

2. "Teacher, teacher, Billy says I look like a baboon!"
-"Shhhh! Just be quiet, comb your face & get back in line."

3. "Teacher, teacher, I keep trying to run, But I only go in circles!"
-"Shhhh! Be quiet or I'll nail your other foot to the floor."

4. "Teacher, teacher, Jimmy won't let go of my ear!"
- "Shhhh! Jimmy please let go of Lizzy's ear. Jimmy, Let go of her ear! Ohh! Okay Jimmy, put that ear down right here and get back to your seat."

5. "Teacher, teacher, why are you pushing the church
 bus into the lake?"
- "Shhhh! You'll wake all the other kids."

6. "Teacher, teacher, my head hurts."
- "Shhhh! Just be quiet and hold that dart board a little bit
higher."

7. "Teacher, teacher, can I go out to recess now?"
- "Shhhh! Just light my cigarette and deal the cards."

8. "Teacher, teacher, Jimmy says my head is too big."
-"Shhhh! Just move your hat out of the bathroom so the other
kids can use it."

9. "Teacher, teacher, is it time for lunch yet?"
- "Shhhh! Just leave the dead squirrel in the bag & be quiet."

10. "Teacher, teacher, I don't think I like swimming."
- "Shhhh! I'll tell you when to get out of that sack."

Memories

A distraught older woman sought out the minister for
counseling. She was concerned that her aging husband kept waking
each morning and asking, "Where am I Catherine?"

"I see," said the minister. "And you are worried that your
husband may be getting Alzheimer's?"

The woman looked a little bit puzzled, before replying,

"Well no. I was just a bit concerned because my name is
Margaret."

Inhaler

The minister's wife gave her husband a small beautifully wrapped box on his birthday. The minister carefully unwrapped it to find what looked to be a small inhaler. Reading the small print on the device, it explained that it contained vitamin E and Viagra.

How unusual, thought the minister? Later he asked his wife why anyone would want to put Viagra in an inhaler?

She embarrassingly explained that she thought it might be helpful, since sex now seemed to be .... mainly in his HEAD.

Mistletoe

There was a certain minister who liked to hang mistletoe above the collection plate at his church.

It was, he stated,

"For those who wanted to kiss their money good-bye!"

New Church

After a particularly long sermon in the congregation's brand new church, a grumpy old deacon was asked about the acoustics in the new church.

"Terrible!" he replied, "I could hear every word the minister said".

10 Warning Signs that the Priest is getting Older

He drops his teeth in the chalice.

He prefers the communion Host 'pureed'.

He is still upset with Martin Luther.

His Oxygen lines keep getting tangled.

He has a bathroom added behind the altar.

He needs a flashlight to find the candles.

He has fortunetellers offering to 'read' his face.

He sponsors and wins church 'belching' contests.

The snacks at church socials are now bran muffins
and prune juice.

He likes to wear his old tie-died robes.

He sits in his rocking chair and can't get it going.

Faith healers

A point to ponder: Have you ever visited the home of
a faith healer? - And been tempted to look in their medicine
cabinet?

Canada

A soft-spoken, pious young priest had just been relocated from a church in northern Canada to one in Florida. When asked about his brief stay at his former church, the man replied that he had gotten along well with everyone there. But, he had been relocated anyway, because of all the trouble he had starting his car on cold mornings.

-He just didn't have the vocabulary "!*%!!&*" for it.

The same priest explained that he knew it was time to move from Canada when he went to take out the garbage one freezing morning - and it just wouldn't go!

Criss-Crossing Over

What do you get when you cross a Jehovah's Witness with a Unitarian Universalist?
...Someone who knocks on your door for no particular reason...

What do you get when you cross a Druid and a Buddhist?
...Someone who worships the tree that is not there...

What do you get when you cross a praying mantis with a termite?
...An insect that says grace before eating the church.

What do you get when you cross a fatalist with a Course in Miracles student?
...Someone who thinks they paid too much for their new car, refuses to do anything about it and is grateful for the lesson.

Breakfast with Jesus

A Christian mother was preparing breakfast for her two sons. The boys started to argue about who should get the first waffle. The mother realized this would be a good opportunity to teach the boys about her faith and said...

"If Jesus was sitting here, He would say, 'let my brother have the first pancake and I will wait.'"

The older of the two boys nodded his shaggy head in understanding and looked gently at his younger brother stating, "Brian, it's your turn to be Jesus."

Excuses

The old priest stopped one of his parishioners as he was exiting the church. He stared at the man with a baleful eye and accused him,
"I heard that you went to the ball game last Sunday instead of coming to church."

"That's a lie!' said the man. "And I have the fish to prove it!"

The Earrings

The old priest was called in to counsel one of the matriarchs of the parish. The proud old grand dame had been married and divorced several times over the years but had remained, throughout it all, a staunch supporter of the church.

This day she was wearing a set of earrings made from the two halves of her last wedding ring. The earring on one lobe read, "WITH ALL" and the other,
"MY LOVE".

The priest commented that the earrings were certainly interesting and made good use of a piece of jewelry that would otherwise lie neglected. And, that by wearing them, she could still cling to some loving memories of her former husband.

"No." she replied, they were just to remind her that if she should ever hear those same words again,

"To let them go in one ear and out the other".

Sin

The old priest was being re-located to a different parish. A crying young woman came up to him after his last scheduled Mass and said,

"Father O'Bunnion, I am going to miss you so much. I didn't even know what sin was until you came here."

The Leaf

A young girl was flipping through the pages of a family bible that she had brought with her to Sunday School. Amongst the pages was a dried up leaf from an old oak tree that had been pressed between the pages.

As she turned to the next page, the leaf fluttered out and landed next to the Sunday School teacher. Looking down, the teacher asked the girl what had fallen.

The little girl thought for a second before answering,

"I think it's Adam's suit."

The Poor

The minister spoke to his Sunday congregation and reminded them that he had advertised that their church would welcome new members from all socio -economic situations - and especially the poor.

And, holding up the nearly empty collection plate - announced sourly, "That they have come."

****

When I was younger, my parents would always tell me to eat and appreciate my food because there were poor 'starving' children in China.

In today's world, I turn on the air conditioner and tell my kids that they should appreciate it more because of the poor 'sweating' kids in China.

The Miser

An old miser had only one daughter. She married a minister and delivered four children of her own. The grandchildren arrived to celebrate the holidays with the old miser. Their smiling faces touched the old man's heart and loosened his purse strings.

When the Christmas holiday ended there was a tear dripping from the old miser's eye as he watched the family leave with their arms filled with the gifts he had purchased for them. He hated to see his loved 'ones' go... also his loved 'five's', 'tens' and 'twenties'.

Poison

A man goes to see his rabbi to complain that he thinks his wife is trying to poison him. The rabbi is shocked and asks the man how this could be. The man is adamant and says,
"I just know that my food doesn't taste right and that she is trying to kill me."

The rabbi tries to reassure him and says that he will talk to the wife and get to the bottom of this so that the man can stop worrying.
The rabbi calls the man back into his office and tells him that having spent several hours with the wife the previous night, he had some advice for him.

"Take the poison."

The Wall

In Jerusalem an old Jewish man had been going to the Wailing Wall to pray twice a day every day for over forty years. A curious tourist asked the man what it was he had been praying for so diligently all these years.
The man answered that he had been praying for peace between the Arabs and the Jews. He had asked that all the hatred stop, and asked that their children be able to live together

in harmony.

The tourist was visibly moved by the old man's faith and asked him how he felt about the power of prayer.

The old man thought for a second and answered,

"It's like talking to a frigging wall!"

Ice Fishing

A recently ordained minister was assigned to a church in northern Michigan. The young man had enjoyed fishing as a young boy in Florida. When he heard that there was something called ice fishing here in Michigan, he decided to give it a try.

He borrowed an ice auger and some fishing gear from the senior minister and headed out to a small pond alone. Trying to be careful of his footing, the young man augured a hole into the ice. He set out his gear and was just sitting down to get comfortable when a deep powerful voice came from above.

"THERE ARE NO FISH UNDER THE ICE."

The minister jumped up at the sound of the voice and looked all around him. But there was no one there. A bit cautiously, he returned to his seat next to his gear. The voice from above spoke again.

"THERE ARE NO FISH UNDER THE ICE."

The astonished man jumped up, looked around once more and asked loudly.

"Is that you God?"

"NO," came the voice, "THIS IS THE RINK MANAGER."

Grave Experience

Two priests were celebrating their recent retirement at a bar in Ireland. They had been drinking quite a bit and one finally excused himself and headed back to the church rectory. It was a snowy night out and on the way back he decides to cut through the church cemetery. He doesn't see an open grave in the inky darkness, trips and falls in.

The second priest finishes telling stories to the other patrons at the bar and then he too leaves to return to the rectory. On his way back he hears a terrible moaning coming from the cemetery and decides to investigate.

The moaning becomes clearer,

"Coldd! Colddd! Ohhh, so Coldddd!"

Looking down into the open grave, the second priest doesn't recognize his friend and only says,

"Of course you're cold. You've managed to kick all the dirt off yourself."

The Minister's Dog

A Baptist minister in Texas had a talking dog of which he was very proud. The dog suddenly disappeared for three weeks. Then, the minister was told that his dog had been seen limping into an old western town using only three legs.

Dragging it's tired, thirsty body and useless fourth leg into a nearby saloon, the dog had sat down on a stool and announced to the patrons,
"I'M LOOKING FOR THE MAN THAT SHOT MY PAW!"

Turbulence

A Catholic priest was taking a cross-country flight to California when the plane ran into some severe in-flight turbulence. The turbulence got even worse and several of the younger passengers were getting frightened.

The stewardess noticed the priest's garments and asked if there was anything the priest could use from his church experience in this moment of crisis to help out.

The priest thought for a second, borrowed the hat from the passenger next to him and took up ... a collection.

Elephants

Four ancient blind Elephants had lived in the jungles of India their entire lives without any contact with man. A young Elephant had just joined the herd and was trying to explain to the four matriarchs what human beings were like.

The explanation (four limbs, a tiny head, mighty machines and many Gods) seemed too incredible to believe, so the four ancient Elephants decided to find out the truth about man by direct experience.

Setting out together with the young Elephant as a guide, they made their way to the nearest village. Here, the young Elephant directed the four to where a young missionary was gathering water.

The first blind elephant stomped her way over to the water, reached down and examined the missionary beneath her with her trunk and declared,
" The young Elephant is wrong. Humans are just flat."

Her three sisters felt the squashed flesh below them and had to agree. Humans were indeed just that ... flat.

The Pilgrim

A wandering pilgrim was caught in a torrential rainstorm in rural England. Soaked to the bone, tired and hungry, he finally noticed a roadside inn ahead called, 'Arthur & the Dragon'.

Shaking the cold rain from his body the pilgrim enters the inn and asks the large forbidding woman at the front desk if there is any room at the inn this evening.

The woman looks back at him without any seeming compassion and says,

"No."

"Perhaps I could get a little something to eat then?

She frowns and says,

"No."

"Then maybe just something warm to drink?"

The woman's frown turns into a grimace of disdain as she answers again,

"No."

About defeated, the pilgrim asks if he might be permitted one last request.

The scowling woman sizes him up for the coup de grace and asks menacingly.

"What?"

"May I please talk to Arthur?'

Jesus & Elvis

Jesus said, "Love thy neighbor".
Elvis sang, "Don't be cruel".

Jesus was the Lord's shepherd.
Elvis dated Cybil Shepard.

Jesus was part of the Divine Trinity.
Elvis's first band was a trio.

Jesus said, "If any man thirsth, let him come to me and drinkith."
Elvis said, "Drinks on me".

Jesus wore white robes.
Elvis wore a white jump suit.

Jesus lived in a state of grace.
Elvis lived in Graceland.

Jesus was resurrected.
Elvis had a famous comeback tour.

Time & Money

In the Jewish tradition there was a wise old man named Izzy Schwartz. One day in prayer, God appeared to Izzy and he asked,

"Yahweh, is it true that for you, a thousand years is only as a minute?"

God replied, "Yes Izzy, that is true."
Izzy then had a second question. He asked,

"Yahweh, is it also true that for you a million dollars is only a penny?"

God replied, "Yes Izzy, that is also true."
With a sly grin and an upturned hand, Izzy then asked,

"Yahweh, as it is only a penny to you, please give me a million dollars."

To which God replied,

"Of course Izzy! It'll just be a minute."

****

Then there was the frugal priest who decided to save a few dollars on signs for the front of his church. At the hardware store he purchased just four letters and placed the four of them on the front of the church spelling 'OPEN'.

Then when he was locking the doors that evening, he moved the last letter to spell 'NOPE.'

Too Raw

A Baptist minister from Texas was visiting New York City for the first time. He joined some friends at a fancy restaurant near Central Park for dinner. They each ordered the largest steak on the menu.

The steaks arrived but the minister looks at his and sends it back saying it is too raw. The waiter takes the steak back to the kitchen. The waiter returns with the steak and tells the minister that the cook assures him the steak is properly cooked.

The minister looks disgustedly at the steak and tells the waiter to take it back again and relay the following message to the cook.

"I'm from Texas and I've often seen cows hurt worse than this. AND THEY RECOVERED!"

Sleeping with Mom

A gruff Lutheran minister in upstate New York returned home from a conference and his wife took him aside. She explained that during his absence, there had been a huge storm and she had let their four children sleep in bed with her because they were frightened.

The minister was appalled. His children were all older than six and the oldest was fourteen. So, the minister gathered his kids and told them that they were much too old to be sleeping with their mother and that in the future, if they were frightened, they merely had to turn to the 23rd Psalm in their bibles.

Two months later, the minister was returning from a church retreat with several members of his congregation. His wife was to meet them all at the train station.

After a long wait, the minister spied his wife and kids in

the crowd. Regrettably, his oldest boy got to him first and announced proudly and loudly that,

"We've got good news Dad. No one slept with Mom while you were away this time!"

Dinner Gossip

The old rabbi was attending the reception following the marriage of a friend's daughter. It was a marriage out of the faith and there were a lot of people present that were new to the rabbi.

As he went through the dinner buffet line, the rabbi noticed a woman on the other side of the line who was particularly unattractive. Not just overweight but poorly groomed, with large hairy facial warts, one over-sized eye and a stooped back.

Fascinated by the grotesque woman, the old rabbi nudged the arm of the man in line next to him and whispered,

"My God, that woman over there is so ugly she may be scaring the little children."

The stranger next to the rabbi stiffened and replied,

"I'll have you know that the woman there, is my wife!"

The old rabbi was caught in his own gossip and now had to try to avoid an embarrassing situation so, he waved his hand to the side and said,

"No, No.... I meant that other younger woman next to your lovely wife."

"That woman sir... is my Daughter!"

Car Trouble

The minister and his wife were sound asleep in their bed at 1am on a snowy winter morning when someone knocked loudly and persistently at the front door. Hoping they would go away, the minister pulled his pillow over his ears. But the knocking continued until his wife finally begged him to go down and see whom it was.

At the front door was an unknown man. The man's hair was tussled as well as his clothing and the smell of alcohol wafted on his breath as he asked,

"G'Evenin sir. I was wonderin if you'd be good enuf to give me a little push?"

The minister replied,

"Don't you know it's 1am in the morning? And you are obviously drunk. Good night." He shut the door loudly and returned to bed.

By the time the minister got back to his bed his conscience started bothering him. Muttering to himself, the minister got on his foul weather gear and grabbed the keys to his 4X4 truck with the tow bar and went back to find the drunk.

The drunken man was no longer at the front door. The minister peered through the drifting snow and saw a dark shape under a tree in the front yard.

"Are you there? I'm ready to give you that push."

An inebriated voice called back,

"I'm over here on the swing. It's about time. Wheeee!"

Got Gas?

A group of nuns who worked at a nursing home together were driving out of town to pick up a new patient at a retirement complex. Before they could get to the rural address, their car ran out of gas.

A friendly farmer passed the women sitting on the side of the road praying. He stopped and offered to drain some gas from his tank for them. But, he had no can to drain the gas into and couldn't get his truck close enough to drain it to their tank directly.

One of the nuns rummaged through the car and found a large bedpan that they had intended to use with their newest patient.

"Will this work, sir?"

"Sure will," replied the farmer. And he proceeded to drain a full gallon of gas into the pan. When he had finished, he bid the nuns a good day and set off to finish his errands.

The nuns thanked the farmer and God for the gift and gently tipped the contents of the pan into the open cap of their gas tank.

At just this moment, a state trooper drove by and took notice of the odd sight. He stopped his car, backed up to the nuns and hollered to them,

"I don't think that's going to work ladies. But, I sure do admire your Faith!"

Swimming

The new minister at the church was very bright but also very lazy. The man's weight had increased over a hundred pounds in less than a year. The senior minister decided to intervene and took the grossly obese man aside.

In his best conciliatory tones he told the young man how much he was appreciated by everyone in the congregation but, how much more effective he might be if he just lost some weight. He would then feel better about himself and be able to participate in more of the church's activities.

The rotund young minister looked up from his couch and explained that exercise didn't 'suit' him. Running hurt his feet, walking bothered his knees and he didn't believe in competition so, most sports were definitely out.

The senior minister wasn't ready to let it go that easily and tried to think of the least difficult form of exercise.

"How about swimming then - even if you just get in the pool regularly, the activity would help melt some pounds off and improve your figure."

The massive young minister blinked his eyes for a second before rejoining,

"Reverend, I don't know that to be a fact - haven't you ever seen a Whale?"

(That same young minister had to take a leave of absence for health reasons later that year. - He caught pneumonia while standing in front of the refrigerator.)

Breakfast in Bed

A Mormon elder had just married a progressively -minded young woman. He suggested that it would be nice if she prepared him breakfast in bed each day. She didn't say anything in reply.

After reading from his favorite part of the Book of Mormon that night, he was about to switch out the house lights. That's when he first noticed the cot.... in their kitchen.... with a muffin and a glass of milk on the counter.... and the little note....'Enjoy Breakfast'.

Spending Money

One minister confided to a friend of his at the annual church retreat,

"I don't know what to do with this new young wife of mine. She's always asking for money. Twenty dollars last week, twenty again yesterday and just this morning she wanted fifty dollars!"

"My gosh," said his friend, "what does she do with all that money?"

The minister scratched his head before replying,

"I don't rightly know. I never give her any."

Ashes to Ashes

A priest was visiting a young woman who h ad recently moved into his parish. In the woman's living room, the priest noted a beautifully carved vase filled with ashes. The priest asked about them and the young woman replied,

"Oh, Those are my father's ashes."

The priest recovered quickly and apologized for any insensitivity explaining,

"I'm so sorry, I didn't know your poor father had passed on."

To which she replied,

"He hasn't. He's just too damn lazy to go into the kitchen for an ashtray."

Dirt to Dirt

A group of scientists who had perfected the science of cloning of different species decided to challenge God to a contest. They would each start at the same time and see who could create a dinosaur first from just a pile of dirt.

God agreed to the contest but when the scientists reached down for a handful of dirt from which to start the contest, God added,

"No. No.... we each have to use only our own dirt. Please put mine down."

(The scientists are still working on that one.)

The Old West

A missionary to the Oregon territories in the 1800's came upon an American Indian brave lying on the ground with his ear pressed into the dirt. A whisper came from the Indian's lips, as the missionary got closer.

"Six men, on horses with carriage and two squaws."

'Wow," said the missionary, "you can tell all that just from listening to the ground?"

"Unh..Unh.." replied the Indian, "They just run over me."

The Island

A priest, a minister and a rabbi were shipwrecked and then marooned on a desert island in the middle of the Indian Ocean. They survived there for over three years by helping one another and eating seafood and coconuts.

Finally, one day a bottle washed up on the island beach. When the rabbi opened the bottle a genie appeared and gratefully offered each of the men one wish that the genie would grant for them.

The rabbi asked immediately that he be allowed to return home to be with his parents, sisters, his wife and their small daughter.

Sha-Zaamm! He was whisked back to his home.

The minister was next and he too wished that he could be back with his family and taste real food again.

Sha-zamm! And the man was returned home to his family.

The priest was next but asked the genie if he could have some time to think before making his wish. The genie agreed and allowed the priest two weeks to think about his wish. The priest took the time and walked back and forth across the small beach thinking.

He was old and he had lived a life of solitude and prayer. He had no family. The only thing he missed was the company of the minister and the rabbi. So, when the genie asked what his wish would be, he said,

"I just want to be back together with my two friends."

Sha-zaam! ... The island reunion was not a happy one...

Prayers

The pretty young girl was overheard praying,

"Dear Lord, I ask nothing for myself. But could you bring my poor suffering mother a rich, handsome young son-in-law."

Jesus

Jesus walked into a small innkeeper's establishment in Jerusalem and threw three nails down on the counter asking,

"Could they put him up for the night?"

Church Bulletin Items

Ladies, don't forget the church rummage sale. It's a chance to get rid of those things not worth keeping around the house. Bring your husbands.

Fund raiser. The ladies of the church have cast off clothing of every kind. They may be seen in the church hall on Saturday.

Don't let worry kill you. Let your church help.

The peace mediation training scheduled for today has been canceled due to a conflict.

Like-new mattress for sale. Slight urine smell.

Please ladies! Lend the pastor your electric girdles for the church's pancake breakfast next week.

The low-self-esteem group will meet this Friday in the church basement. Please use the back door.

Weight watchers group will meet at 7. Please use the large double doors at the side entrance.

Our Sunday school teens will be performing "Hamlet" next month. The congregation is invited to attend this tragedy.

Prayer and fasting retreat this weekend. Cost for attending includes all meals.

Morning sermon "Jesus. Walking on the water."
Evening sermon "Looking for Jesus."

Our friend Phyllis is in the hospital for an operation and is having difficulty sleeping. She requests copies of Reverend Tim's sermons.

Tryouts for the church choir next week. They need all the help they can get.

The evening sermon will be "What is Hell." Please come early and listen to the choir.

A bean supper will be held Sunday night in the church hall. Stay to listen to the music afterwards.

The chocolate walnuts will no longer be served at church potlucks because they are not everything they were cracked up to be.

Fred donated the new loudspeaker to the congregation - in memory of his wife.

Church Definitions

Amen - the part of the prayer everybody knows.

Incense - holy smoke.

Magi - The most famous trio to attend a baby shower.

Church bulletin - church air conditioning.

Oyster - sprinkling your conversation with too many Yiddish expressions.

Inner Peace - A short attention span.

Zen Gifts

The Zen student realized that the master's birthday was the next day. He went into a deep meditation to find the answer to what would be the perfect gift.

The next day as the entire monastery was celebrating the Zen master's birthday with cake and goodies, the young student presented the master with a beautifully wrapped box.

The master took the box and removing the colorful wrapping, found it empty inside. Putting it down, he spoke to the student.

"You are thoughtless for giving me this meaningless gift."

To which the student replied,

"Thank you."

Glad Wrap

The church's spiritual counselor had an appointment to see a man from the congregation. This man was rumored to be having some major emotional crises in his life.

The disturbed man arrived wearing only an undergarment made of clear Glad Wrap. The man didn't stay long and left quickly in a huff, when the counselor declared,

"I can clearly see your nuts."

How To Make God Chuckle

1. Say you 'think the doctor cured you'.

2. Tell him 'your plans'.

3. Say to anything 'this is mine'.

4. Say to any situation 'I understand".

5. Complain that today was 'hot'.

Stray Cats

The church deacon found that there were stray cats multiplying in the neighborhood and taking up residence in the church. The man did his best to keep them out, but they just kept sneaking back in and breeding until there were just more and more cats.

He finally got the minister's permission to have the church fumigated. This worked for a short time but by the following year, the cats were back in residence.

A visiting minister offered to help out. Within a week, all of the cats were gone and never seen again. When asked how he had accomplished this seeming miracle, the minister replied,

"It was easy. I just baptized the whole lot of them and made them members of the church."

Lot and his Wife

A Christian father was reading from the Bible to his young children one evening. He told them about the man named 'Lot' who was warned by God to take his wife and flee from the wicked twin cities of Sodom and Gomorrah. Lot's wife had turned to look back and was turned into a pillar of salt.

The kids looked suitably impressed by the story but the smallest child still wanted to know what happened to the 'flea'.

Bumper Stickers

'Please don't squeeze the Shaman.'

'Be Modest and be Proud of it'

Guidelines for Ministers visiting New York City

1. The city does not employ 'wallet inspectors'.

2. It's considered bad manners to lie down in someone else's chalk outline.

3. If you see something that looks like chili but doesn't smell like chili - it isn't chili.

4. Cab drivers frown on 'blessings' as tips.

The Curse

An old man approaches a priest and asks him to remove a terrible curse that has been plaguing him for over 40 years. The priest agrees to help the man and asks what words were used to place the curse upon him.

The old man thanks the priest, sighs deeply and speaks the dreaded words,

"I now pronounce you man and wife."

Knowing your Mate

Fred and his wife June were in the minister's office for some marital counseling. Fred thought the relationship was fine but June complained that they never talked.

The minister explained to both of them how important it is to communicate and get to know about those things that are important to each other.

Fred just laughed and said that they talked plenty and his wife was just making a mountain out of a molehill.

Noticing June's growing anger, the minister asked Fred if he could name and describe June's favorite flower.

"Sure, sure," said Fred. He thought for a moment and then leaned over to whisper in June's ear,

"It's Pillsbury, isn't it?"

And thus began Fred's life of celibacy.

Towering Story

A well-known TV evangelist was known for embellishing the truth on occasion in his zeal to make new converts. A news reporter felt compelled to question his latest claim - that he would be using the devotee's donations to build a ten thousand story building in God's name. It turned out to be the truth.... but he hadn't mentioned it was a LIBRARY.

Africa

Two young missionaries had been captured by a wild uncivilized African tribe of cannibals. The men were tightly bound, stripped naked and placed in a huge pot of water.

As all seemed hopeless and the fire beneath the pot grew warmer, the first commented optimistically to his half-cooked friend...

"At least they'll get a taste of religion."

****

Two cannibals were sitting around the fire complaining about their lives. The first says,
'I hate my mother-in-law."
The second replies,
"So, try the potatoes."

Making Babies

Little Reggie came home from school today with a big smirk on his face. The minister's wife was visiting and asked him what he had learned at school that day.
He replied,

"How to make babies."

Reggie's mother and the minister's wife both blanched and only recovered from their shock when he added,

"First you drop the 'y' and then you add 'ies'."

Spelling

The newly arrived minister had fired the church secretary. A friend asked the minister why he had fired the poor woman, who was well-liked in the congregation.

"She kept asking me how to spell the simplest words for her. This went on day after day. I couldn't take it any longer."
The friend nodded in understanding.

"Yes, I can see how that could be very annoying."

"Annoying isn't the half of it. It was positively embarrassing to keep saying, 'I don't know' all the time!"

Professor 'God'

Professor 'God' was recently fired from a major university because he:

Had only one major publication.

Some doubt he even wrote it himself.

When part of his 'experiment' wasn't turning out right, he drowned the sample.

He rarely came to class and just told his students to read the book.

It was said that he had his son teaching some of his classes.

He expelled his first two students for learning.

His office hours were very limited and held only on a mountaintop.

The Vatican

Several priests were gathered together at a Catholic conference in Zurich. One of the priests asked the others if they had heard the latest Vatican joke.

A tall dark-haired priest in back strode forward and proclaimed pompously,

"No, but I'll have you know that 'I' work at the Vatican."

Rather than getting silent, the first priest continued with a whisper,

"That's okay. I'll tell it veryyy... veryyyy.... slowly."

AA Meeting

A retired priest was standing up at the front of a packed Alcoholics Anonymous meeting telling the story of the destruction alcohol had wrought in his life.

"The shame. The disrespect. The lies. Is there anything in the world that can make a person as miserable as too much drink?"

To which a shrill voice sang up from the back of the room, "TOO MUCH THIRST?"

Heaven

At the end of the Sunday School lesson, the minister came in and asked how many children would like to go to Heaven. Eager young arms shot up all over the classroom until just one remained unraised.

The minister came over to little Reggie and asked him if there was something wrong. Didn't he want to go to heaven?

Little Reggie himmmed & hawwwed, then spoke,

"Sure Reverend, eventually... but the way you asked the question, I thought you might be making up a busload right now."

Space Travel

The U.S. Space Agency had recently released the news that it intended to send a new expedition to explore the planet Mars.

To show the world the power and prestige of the Vatican, the pope declared that the Catholic Church would be sending an even more remarkable expedition to explore the Sun.

U.S. scientists expressed shock and sent a delegation to Rome to ask how the papal scientific team was planning to deal with the perils of extreme heat and radiation. They received the following written note:

"We will be sending our expedition at night!"

Crazy?

A member of the Hari Krishna's was sent by his wife to seek counseling from an Episcopal minister. The minister did his best to make the young man feel comfortable and then asked him why he thought his wife felt he needed counseling.

The Hari Krishna scratched his bald scalp and replied that he wasn't sure - but he thought it might have something to do with his preference for sandals over closed-toe shoes.

"Why that's no problem," exclaimed the minister.
"As a matter of fact, I prefer sandals myself.

"Really," replied the young man,
"Do you like yours boiled, smoked or pan-fried?"

Smooth Talker

A rather slow, shy, single minister named Reverend Clem had just been transferred to a new congregation where one of the local spinsters had taken a romantic interest in the young man. The following was overheard at the annual church picnic when the lady managed to get herself alone with the reverend.

"Reverend Clem, do you think I'm pretty?"
"Ahhh....yup."

"Reverend Clem, do you think I'm fun to be around and make you happy?"

"Ahhh....yup."

"Reverend Clem, do you think my lips are as soft as flower petals and my eyes as enchanting as an evening sunset?"

"Ahhh Yup."

"Oh Reverend Clem! You do say the most romantic things."

Yale

The bishop was interviewing several candidates for the seminary. One man was particularly impressive. Good looking, young, well-groomed and with an air of competence. Perfect material for the priesthood.

The bishop then asked if the man had any education beyond high school and the answer was,
"Yale".

"Wonderful," said the bishop. "a fine school. I have some good friends who've attended there. And, by the way, what is your name my son?"

"Yackson."

Garlic Diet

The Indian Guru decided to put a group of his over-weight western followers on a garlic diet. They could continue to eat whatever they wanted, but must add garlic to every food item.

He knew that when they returned home that they wouldn't have lost any weight but that their friends would think they looked thinner.... from a distance!

Adam and Eve

When Adam's children grew up, they asked him why they no longer lived in the paradise of Eden. He whispered that their mother had, 'Eaten them out of house and home'.

Irish Priest

The old Irish priest was visiting the home of one of his parishioners and over dinner a small boy on the other side of the table kept staring at the priest. When the priest took the boy aside and asked about the meaning of the intent stare, the boy replied,

"I just was waiting to see if Mommy was right and if you could really, 'drink like a fish'.

Blood Drive

The dour bishop was rarely seen out of his quarters. But this day he called a church meeting and was exhorting the priests at the cathedral to become more involved in the community, to work to improve the image of the church, to make a difference!

Then he proclaimed the coming month as 'We Give' February. The cathedral would open its doors to the community and the first function would be a community blood drive.

The bishop proclaimed that he would lead the way by donating the first pint of blood.

To which a dubious priest in back warily replied, "I wonder WHOSE?"

Nice Tan

The bishop was visiting a beachside community and was invited to a welcoming party down by the ocean. He had been out of the sun and covered by his cloak for many years and his skin was very pale. To avoid getting sunburn, he went to the drugstore and asked for a strong sunscreen product.

The clerk offered him a tube of SPF 14 cream and explained that it offered all day protection for most people. The bishop looked at the tube and asked if there was anything stronger.

The clerk rummaged on his shelf and produced a tube of SPF 32 cream. The bishop looked at this tube very carefully and asked,

"Is this the strongest sun protection you have?"

The clerk went into the back of the store and returned with a large tube marked SPF 100 and told the bishop,

"This is the strongest sun screen we carry. It is guaranteed to prevent any burning."

The happy bishop thanked the clerk, paid for the SPF 100 tube and headed for the beach party. In the bathhouse changing room the bishop removed his robes and opened his new sunscreen product. There was some surprise on his face as the tube was opened and..... a jacket fell out!

Burial 'Rites'

A Methodist farmer died in an accident while his minister was out of town. The family couldn't wait for his return and asked the local priest if he would conduct the service for their father.

The priest was unsure and said he would find out from the bishop. He wrote the bishop the following note.

"Bishop, can I bury a Methodist?"

The bishop sent the following note in reply.

"Yes, Please bury all the Methodists you can."

Potpourri

"Did you hear Ralph snoring in church this morning?"
"Sure did - he woke me up twice!"

"Minister, my wife doesn't understand me. Does yours?"
The minister. "I don't think she even knows you."

A less than tidy monk with poor hygiene was coaxed by the other monks to buy some 'odor-eaters' for his sandals. It didn't work out. They 'ate' for a minute, and then they threw up.

The minister who was caught spending too much time rehearsing his sermons was admonished for, 'practicing what he preaches'.

The priest was upset when he found out that one of the donated books for the church rummage sale was titled 'Pathways to Petting'.
That was, until someone showed him it was part of an..... Encyclopedia.

The church was having a funeral for the man who had invented the 'hokey pokey' dance. The service went fine but something strange happened when it came time for the burial... First they put his left foot in.....

A friend asked lonely Lisa if she had ever dated.

"Sure," she replied,

"I've even been asked to get married."

"By whom".

She answered sadly, "Mom and Dad."

The new priest goes into a barroom but orders only water. Seeing the tough-looking characters around him, he tells the barkeep loudly- "But put it in a dirty glass".

What's the difference between an Irish wedding and an Irish funeral?
-One drunk Irishman.

Our latest statistics show that the Catholic Church must be doing something right - their priests have the lowest divorce rate in the country!

The rich old church elder was believed to be loosening his purse strings when he pledged $500,000. to the church building fund. At the end of the year, the minister still had not received the money and sent a note telling the man his pledge was a year old. The reply came back a week later - 'Happy Birthday.'

More statistics: 60% of Americans believe in miracles - 20% of these go to church, the other 40% put their faith in the lottery.

Heard in A Catholic confessional booth: "Father I missed Sunday Mass because on the way I had rear end trouble, the car swerved because of it - causing me to have an accident."

The Catholic Church, in an effort to keep up with the times has added a new confessional booth to speed things up - for those with three sins or less.

God heals - doctors collect the fees.

Honesty pays - but not enough to suit most people.

Which is worst, death or taxes? At least death isn't an annual event.

Without sin, there would be a problem with unemployed clergy.

A young woman once asked about Buddha if that was really his 'Christian' name.

The minister explained that the secret to his long successful marriage was that he and his wife took two nights a week to go out to a nice dinner followed by dancing and cocktails...
"My wife goes on Monday, I go on Fridays."

The priest teases the rabbi about trying 'ham' some time to see what he is missing. The rabbi says he is waiting for the right time. "And when might that be?"
"At your wedding."

My friend is an Agnostic dyslexic insomniac - he stays up all night wondering if there is a 'dog'.

The Baptist minister's wife got her birth control pills mixed up with her Valium. They now have twenty children - but she just doesn't care.

'Our Lady of Procrastination' holds its services on Tuesday afternoons.

Retirees are mentioned in the Bible in the story about the 'multitude that loafs and fishes'.

What do you call a pair of people who doubt the very existence of God? ... Diagnostic.

The young minister was an incurable optimist. One day he was asked if there was anything positive about getting Alzheimer's disease. After some thought he replied...
"You are always meeting new people."

Our Church is open to all denominations - but it prefers 10's and 20's.

Love of money is the root of all evil. That's why instead of loving it, we are just trying to 'live with it'.

Ethics Class

A young man was taking a class in ethics at the seminary. The instructor asked him what he would do if he saw two trains approaching each other on the same train track - would he say a prayer, go for help or try to throw the switch lever himself?

The young man replied that he would try to throw the switch himself.

"Fine," said the instructor, "but what would you do if the lever was jammed shut?"

The young man said he would take his shirt off and wave it to warn the on-coming trains.

"Fine," replied the instructor, "but what if it was dusk and the train engineers wouldn't be able to see you?"

"In that case, I would send for my parish priest."

"Your priest? And what could he do?"

"Nothing. He just loves to watch train wrecks."

Facelifts

The bishop was only in his sixties but many years in the sun as a boy had given him the hangdog wrinkles of a much older man. Not wanting to appear vain, he secretly went to an unlicensed surgeon while on vacation to get a face-lift.

The operation was a disaster and his tightened skin began burning almost immediately. By the next morning open, infected wounds had appeared all over his face and he was taken to a hospital.

A plastic surgeon was forced to graft new skin onto his face after the infections were healed. The bishop returned home finally after a month's absence.

His wife admired his now-healed face and together they offered up a prayer of gratitude.

After the prayer his wife had to ask,

"Darling, where did they get the skin to repair all that damage?"

"I don't know," said the bishop, "But every time I start to feel tired... my face wants to sit down."

Long Distance Calls

The newly ordained minister was also newly-married. He had just begun his ministry with a small town congregation and money was in short supply.

When the couple's first phone bill arrived, the minister sat back in shock. His wife had run up over a hundred dollars in phone calls to her mother back in Tulsa.

He took his young wife aside and explained their financial situation to her and emphasized how it would be necessary to write letters instead of calling her mother so often.

It was disconcerting that evening then, to hear his wife dialing on the phone just as he was working on his Sunday sermon. But he didn't want to jump to any conclusions as he called out,

"Darling, who are you calling?"

"It's okay dear. I'm just calling for the correct time."

The minister breathed a sigh of relief and was about to sink back into his chair when he had an awful thought and got up to hear his wife say,

"Hello mom, what time is it?"

Naughty

A 'hell-fire' preacher asked his Sunday School class if they knew where little boys and girls went if they are naughty?

Little Reggie piped up first, "To the barn hayloft?"

Trophy Wife

The minister looked out over his Sunday service and saw the richest and oldest member (about 76) of the congregation sitting in the front row with a beautiful young blonde woman hanging all over him. After the service, he took the elderly gent aside and asked about the young woman.

The old man cackled and proudly announced that she was his new wife. The minister was astonished. Then he thought about how the old man had sold cars for a living for many years and.... could there have been some deception involved in this unequal partnership?

So, he asked the old guy outright,
"Did you lie to that young woman and tell her you were only 66?

"No minister. I actually smudged the truth a bit in the other direction. I told her I was 96."

Grandchildren

In a small local church it was noticed when a sweet white - haired grandmother placed twice her usual offering into the weekly collection basket. The minister sought the woman out later and thanked her for her generosity. He couldn't help asking the reason for it. She answered with a smile,

"It is because my grandchildren are finally coming to visit me - and I'm so grateful."

Two weeks later the same grandmother is noticed increasing her offering by a factor of four. Again, the minister seeks her out for an explanation.

"They just left."

Complaints

The old rabbi went to the doctor's office and complained that he was having trouble reading from the Talmud aloud at his synagogue.

"And what do you think is the problem?"

"I'm pretty sure it's this," he replied pointing to his nose and what appeared to be an orange carrot growing out of his left nostril.

"My Goodness," exclaimed the doctor, "I've never seen this before. You must be pretty upset."

"You bet I am," stammered the angry rabbi, "I planted radishes!"

The Faith Healer

A famous faith healer was seated next to a priest on the train. The faith healer asked the priest how he was feeling.

The priest replied that he was fine, but he had a younger brother who was very sick.

The faith healer contradicted the priest saying,

"Your brother isn't sick. He only thinks he's sick. Let him know this, and the power of his Mind will make him well."

The priest thanked him for his advice and they parted at the next station.

Three months later, the faith healer recognized the same priest sitting alone as he boarded the train. He joined the priest and with a beaming smile asked,

"How is that brother of yours doing."?

"Not so good," replied the priest, "Now he thinks he's dead."

Ambrosia

The minister was telling his congregation about some of the Old Testament stories. This day he mentioned a biblical character who had over a hundred wives and concubines - all of whom he fed with ambrosia.

An older gentleman in the back perked up and asked loudly

,
"Never mind what he fed THEM. What did HE eat?"

Norse Gods

Thor, the Norse God of thunder, jumped onto his favorite horse and went out for a long ride around Valhalla. He came back from his ride and handed the reins of his stallion to his new baby - faced groomsman.
Feeling vigorous, Thor thumped his chest and bellowed for the world to hear, "I am Thor!"

To which his frail groomsman replied,
"Of course you are, you forgot your thaddle, thilly."

Consideration

The new church ministry in a large town was meeting temporarily in the high-rise upstairs apartment of one of its members. The sign next to their little altar read,

'Do under others, as you would have them do under you.'

Mindfulness

An older priest chastised a new brother monk who was cleaning the urinals at the monastery in a lackadaisical way. It seemed he couldn't keep his mind 'in the gutter'.

Perspectives

There was a new chapel being built at the monastery. All the monks were helping by moving bags of cement. The bishop watched the industrious monks dragging the heavy bags two at a time through the church hall. All except Brother Lazwell. He carried only one sack on each trip. The bishop asked him why? "I guess the other monks are too lazy to make two trips."

The Elderly

An elderly priest has retired to a small Florida town. He walks by a massage parlor every day and finally decides to go in to experience this thing called 'massage'.

The female masseuse on duty sees a frail old retired priest come in, asks him to sit on the massage table and out of curiosity asks him how old he is.

"I'm 94 years old."

"Wheww!" says the masseuse. "You've just about had it."

"Oh, sorry," says the priest, "How much do I owe you."

Painful Experience

Two ten-year-old boys were talking about circumcision. One was scheduled to be circumcised the following week and wanted to find out what to expect. The other shared that he had been circumcised when he was three months old.

"Do you remember much about it? Did it hurt?"

"Well, I don't remember a lot. But I do know I wasn't able to walk for a year afterwards."

Greed

A professed bigamist was asked to leave the Catholic Church because he couldn't be allowed to,

'Have his Kate and Edith too.'

Cross Words

A member of the church's faithful had recently died. And, as the man was a crossword puzzle devotee during life, the minister had him buried six feet down and three across.

Palm Sunday

The Sunday before Easter is called Palm Sunday in the Catholic Church. After each Palm Sunday Mass the attendees are allowed to take home a small 'blessed' palm frond to keep at home and to burn with special prayers.

Little Billy was only four years old and didn't know about this tradition. He was sick on Palm Sunday and stayed home from church with his older sister. When the rest of the family arrived home carrying their palm fronds, little Billy was curious and asked what they were for?

His parents started to explain that people had held them over Jesus' head as he walked by...

But before they could continue with the story, Billy jumped up furiously and interrupted with,

"Darn! The first Sunday I ever miss... And 'He' shows up."

Mood Ring

The Minister had grown up in the seventies and when he saw a mood ring at the flea market, he purchased it for his 'moody' wife. His wife was unimpressed with the gift but wore it anyway. The next day her friend asked her about the ring.

"My husband says it is called a 'mood ring'. All I know is that when I am in a good mood it turns blue. And, when I am in a bad mood, it leaves a red mark on his forehead."

Gospel of the Egg

On Easter Sunday the minister had seated all the children in the congregation in the front row pew so that he could include them in the sermon. He watched with delight as the children Ohhhhed & Ahhhhed as he waved a colorful Easter bunny in front of them.

At the end of his sermon he produced a large pink Easter egg and held it out for all to see. Before opening it, to distribute the candies inside, He asked one little boy if he could guess what was inside the egg.

This little boy had three older sisters and all he could think to reply was, "Pantyhose?"

A Dinner Prayer

The priest asked little Billy in the confessional if he had remembered to say a prayer each day before every meal.

Little Billy replied,

"No Father, We don't have to. My mother's a good cook."

Section Three

Sound Familiar?

Puns and Groaners

"Make a joyful noise unto the Lord ... and make it Laughter."

Quickies

Father O'Brupt was giving Sister Ruth a ride home from church on his Vespa motor scooter. He had a bit of a reputation as a speed demon and Sister Ruth kept her eyes closed as he wheeled around successive curves. Father O'Brupt didn't see the bump in the road as he hit it - and then continued on Ruthlessly.

There was a clumsy young monk who was assigned a job at the monastery making reading glasses for the older monks. One day he slipped while working on the lens grinder and made a spectacle of himself.

The following week they put the same monk to work in the kitchen helping the cook. But he backed into a meat grinder and got a little behind in his work.

This wasn't working out, so they put the monk in the basement to help out the weaver-monk. There, things were going well until the loom for the upholstery fabric caught the sleeve of his hassock and pulled him violently inside. But don't worry... He's completely 'recovered' now.

A minister in Upstate New York was praying for an early Spring because he couldn't take 'snow' for an answer.

A cannibal was expelled from bible school for buttering up his teacher.

Have you heard about the terrible crime spree that seems to be striking our cities? Yesterday two peanuts were walking to church and one was a-salted.

Did you hear about the new fund-raiser at the Methodist Church? They combined a seafood buffet with a dance contest. The minister made a thousand dollars profit and in each, he pulled a mussel.

Two technology junkies decided to get married and combine their households. Neither wanted to give up their big screen TV's or their huge satellite dishes, so they kept them both.

Their marriage ceremony wasn't much to speak about but the 'reception' was brilliant.

The young woman's family failed to make a donation to the church after the parish priest performed an exorcism – so the poor woman was re-possessed.

Then, there was the missionary sent to convert the savages in darkest Africa. He showed up late for a special dinner with the cannibal tribe and was given the cold shoulder.

They are having a funeral today for a dead Angel. It was said that the Angel died of harp failure.

A Unity Minister was visiting Australia for the first time. As he crossed the road, a motor scooter struck him from behind and knocked him unconscious. When he woke up in the hospital in pain and wrapped in bandages he tremblingly asked the nurse,

"Was, Was ... I brought in here to die?"

"No," said the nurse, "you were brought in here yesterdye."

Gandhi walked barefoot most of his life. He fasted until he weighed very little and when he did eat, it was a very strange organic diet that left his breath smelling of garlic. He described himself as a super-calloused fragile mystic hexed by halitosis.

Then, there was the Buddhist monk who didn't want the dentist at the monastery to use Novocain when he pulled the monk's teeth because he wanted to transcend dental medication.

The well-versed bible scholar was in the hospital recovering from a bad case of the flu. While there, he received a letter addressed to the 'ill literate'.

I've started a new organization for those that don't like to attend church. It's called the 'Seventh-Day Absentists'.

An ill minister's doctor advised her to bath in milk three times a week. So, the next day the woman requested that the milkman deliver eighty gallons of milk to the church. The milkman asked her,

"Do you want that pasteurized?"

"No," she replied, "just up to my chin."

Did you hear about the Muslim prince who lived in a remote part of the Arabian Desert? He went by himself to the holy city of Mecca, had a mystical vision and then returned home early to visit his harem.

His early arrival caused his wives to let out 'a terrific sheik.'

A new bird species has taken up residence in the eaves of the Mission San Juan Capistrano. They have named it the 'Gulp' because it looks like a larger version of the Swallow.

The missionary was trying to help a sobbing cannibal.

"What's wrong?' inquires the missionary.

"I passed my brother in the jungle yesterday."

The minister feared there would be a major crisis in the church when news leaked out that there had been some nudity at the church's last family retreat. But nothing transpired, as there was 'very little coverage'.

The monastery's barbershop was considered a popular place to hang out on hot summer days because it was hair-conditioned.

In the Catholic Church, Communion crackers were now being used again for the Eucharist after being a 'wafer' a while.

There was a Muslim tailor who didn't like to charge for his services because he liked to work 'off the cuff'.

He remained a tailor because he 'seamed' to do so well.

For a parting gift on his way to Mecca, he asked only for a thimble because he didn't want to get 'stuck' without one.

The new church minister had worked with the circus before his ordination. He maintained a habit of walking on a tightrope that he constructed outside his house to relieve stress. But, his congregation still referred to him as 'high-strung'.

And, even with his tightrope walking, the new church job kept the minister uptight much of the time. He even made the yearly 'best-stressed' list.

The Catholic Church recently relaxed some of it's bans on contraceptive devices and instead, is focusing more on proper diet or, as we call it - 'girth control'.

The young friar claimed to have been kidnapped by aliens and taken in a lighter than air craft to a secret city in the clouds. But the rest of the brothers at the monastery thought it was just 'a lot of balooney'.

The new alarm clock at the monastery didn't seem to be waking the monks up in time for morning meditation so, one of the monks brought in a huge old bell clock. Now the monks are able to 'rise and chime'.

A Tibetan monk was traveling through Europe and he stopped in Hungary to establish a mission to help some of the suffering Catholics in its capital city. To many he was considered a saint, but to the local priest, he was a 'Buddha Pest'.

The Dalai Lama had been kneeling in meditation all day with several of his followers. Getting up finally, he went to a nearby cabinet and took out a Scrabble game so that they all could 'sit down for a spell'.

Brother John worked in the monastery garden all day. At night he would only look at picture books about flowers and horticulture. His fellow monks were surprised when they heard that the local literary society had nominated him for a prize for being a very 'good weeder'.

A crafty monk finally found the missing can of lubricating oil for the extra wheelchairs in the church pantry. Until then, their disabled visitors had just been squeaking by.

The supply of tanning oil at the Muslim mosque was nearly empty. But the Arab caretaker told the faithful not to worry. They wouldn't run out because they only used it on Sun -days.

The Greek Orthodox priest left his church in Greece and moved to America because he was tired of listening to lyres.

The young monk left the monastery to seek his way in the world. He had never held a job but, looking through the newspaper want ads, he was able to apply for work at a large hotel in town because he could honestly state that he was 'inn -experienced'.

Several Arab mullahs arrived in Las Vegas for the lavish wedding of a Saudi prince. As the happy couple walked up the aisle, the mullahs threw 'dice' at the couple instead of rice. A security guard tried to explain that our tradition involved rice, not 'dice', despite Las Vegas' reputation as a gaming town.

The mullahs looked back at the security guard and said that they did indeed understand our traditions but that they only wanted the couple to have a little 'par -a-dice' here on Earth.

A man walks into a Catholic Church with a piece of asphalt under his arm and gets in line for communion. The man receives his communion wafer and asks the priest for a second. The priest asks why? The man says he wants one for the road.

Also in the same communion line is a jumper cable. When the cable gets to the front of the line the priest says, "Okay, I'll serve you. Just don't start anything!"

The monks at the monastery were complaining that the sausages at the evening meal tasted strange. One end tasted like pork but the other tasted like breadcrumbs. The monk who was doing the cooking explained that in these difficult economic times, it was harder to 'make both ends meat'.

A clergyman noted for his poor memory was warmly greeted on the street by a member of his congregation. Shaking the man's hand, he returned the greeting with,

"I can't remember your name but your faith is familiar."

The Baptist minister placed his teenage son in a weight -training program because he wanted him to spend time in a more 'uplifting' environment.

Church termites never die. They just go on living happily every rafter.

There was the nun who went to sleep every night wrapped in an old shroud. It became a very bad habit.

The Baptist minister in Texas ordered ice cream with his pie for dessert because he wanted to 'remember the a la mode.'

The same Texas minister recently was granted a divorce from his wife after he found his 'Dear and an interloper at play'.

The bishop went on a diet because he was 'thick and tired of it'.

A Chinese Zen master was speaking at the monastery when all the lights in the building went out. The master bowed his head and asked all the accolades in the audience to raise their hands high in the air.

The lights immediately came back on thereby proving the old saying that,
'Many hands make light work.'

Our favorite minister had a special drawer for all his bills marked 'Due unto others.'

The old rabbi had just finished wolfing down his entire meal. Suddenly, he looked up with concern and tugged at his wife saying,

"Becca, I, I tink I svallowed a bone."

"Are you choking Samuel?"

"No, I'm serious!"

How did the rabbi keep his bagel from running away?
He put lox on it.

The rabbi was called in to bless a new Jewish restaurant that was opening soon. It was going to serve kosher food from India. They named it the 'New Delhi-catessan'.

Just before the great flood, Noah was heard remarking ungrammatically, "Now I herd everything."

The minister liked to publish as much gossip as possible in the church bulletin because he wanted to 'write others wrongs.'

The same minister decided to take three collections at every Sunday service instead of one because he didn't want to 'put all his begs in one basket'.

Two Buddhist monks are meditating outside on a very cold night in Tibet with only small oil lamps for light and warmth. The head Lama visits the first monk and finds the man sitting in prayer nearly frozen, his teeth are chattering and the wick in his lamp is completely burned out.

The Lama replaces the lamp wick, lights the flame anew and rubs circulation back into the man's shoulders. He pats the young meditator on the head and goes to find the second monk.

This man's lamp is also expired. But, the man is soundly asleep under his blanket. The Lama rudely kicks the sleeping man awake and then turns to leave him.

"But Lama, my lamp went out and I have no heat."

"Sorry," said the Lama as he left, "there is no wick for the rested".

A new priest was visiting an insane asylum in the state of Wyoming. It was the Christmas season and all the inmates were out in the hospital yard. Several of the men had on lovely velvet choir capes and were singing to their fellow inmates.

The priest was impressed by the wonderful rhythm and the quality of the men's voices. Oddly, the singers each held a red apple that they struck with a long stick in time to the music.

Approaching the doctor in charge, the priest complimented the director for the quality of the music program. He even suggested that his church would love to host the singing inmates in the future.

"By the way," he asked, "what do you call this singing group, so that I can list them in our church bulletin?"

"Surely that's obvious," replied the director, "they're the 'Moron tap-an-apple choir'."

Lutheran pastors in Germany are called German Shepherds.

The most successful banker in the bible was the
Egyptian pharaoh's daughter because she went down
to the Nile River and drew out a little prophet.

Ministers in Texas always chose to die with their boots on so, that they won't hurt themselves when they 'kick the bucket.'

Did you hear about the Buddhist cow that wanted to achieve nirvana? It was dyslexic and it chanted its mantra 'OOOMMM'.

Then, there was the dyslexic rabbi who went around saying "YO!"

There was a very poor, but proud, English Episcopal monastery. For dinner each night they served.........'Gruel Wellington'.

There was the near-sighted monk who walked right through the monastery screen door and 'strained' himself.

Our minister just returned from a vacation to Scotland. He brought back with him some very tasty cheese for the after-service social. When asked what type of cheese it was, he claimed it to be...'Loch Ness Muenster'.

The guru left the New Year's Eve masquerade party early because he was having a hard time telling the...'good guise from the bad'.

The monastery's organic vegetable garden featured a little hand carved sign stating..."We till it the way it is".

There was a monk who started wearing bib overalls and picking his teeth with a straw. When asked why, he said he believed in 'REINCORNATION' - coming back in the next life as a hillbilly.

Little Reggie was obstinate and silly. His sister told him he had to stop giggling and fooling around during the church service. He responded,

"Who's going to make me?"

His sister pointed to the back of the church and whispered,

"The 'hushers'".

Our church recently started a twelve-step program for compulsive talkers ... its called 'On-and-On Anon'.

An elderly woman confessed to her priest that she was having a recurring dream in which she was painting everything in sight with gold paint. The priest told her not to worry. It was only her 'gilt complex'.

Our interdenominational get-together and prayer meeting attracted an especially large attendance this year. Some say it was because of the new promotional flyer that proclaimed ... 'Get to know the opposite sects'.

What did the minister's wife do after her favorite cat was crushed by a truck while trying to cross the street? She sat there with a long puss.

When the minister finished a very long sermon last Sunday - there was a great 'awakening'.

Atheism is a non-prophet organization.

A new group is forming that raises consciousness and one's cholesterol levels at the same time. It's called 'Tex - Mexistentialism'.

Female ministers visiting Arab countries have long been encouraged to wear skirts that are unfashionably long. Because, they cover a 'multitude of shins'.

The favorite Christmas carol at the Christian nudist camp was 'Stark the Herald Angels Sing'.

The name of the weight lifting team at the fundamentalist Southern Baptist church was the...'Brawn Again Christians'.

The neighboring town's Congregational church had a new furnace installed. Its members began referring to themselves as... 'Warm Again Christians'.

Not to be outdone, the Baptist church downriver enticed a famous hairdresser to join their congregation and they are now known as the...'Shorn Again Christians'.

A little Catholic nun named Grace was fond of saying her prayers as she walked the pattern in the church's labyrinth. She soon picked up the nickname ...'A-Mazing-Grace'.

A devote young monk went on a diet of prunes and prune juice. Soon, he was spending most of his time in the monastery bathroom. The other monks thought he was crazy. But, he felt he was experiencing an... en-lighten-ment.

The young monk's friend accidentally stuck his finger into the electrical socket while changing a bulb thus, experiencing his own en-lighten-ment.

Confucius says: 'He who pass wind in church, sit in own pew.'

There was a wacky female Buddhist named Anna who sought enlightenment by going around insulting everyone in her path. She soon became known as...'A Lot of Nerve-Anna'.

Anna's brother Carl was also a devout Buddhist. But, because he was overly absorbed with his computer, the master joked that he was seeking 'Nerd-vana'.

Our favorite Buddhist Zen master is named M.T. Ness.

A Southern Baptist minister we know has a habit of spending his Sunday afternoons at the automobile races. He says he doesn't gamble but just goes to experience the...'rev-elation'.

What do you call nuns who walk in their sleep?
-Roaming Catholics.
What do you call nuns who have sex change operations?
-Trans-Sisters.

What did the policeman in the front church pew say when he saw a spider crawl down the priest's neck?
-You're under a vest!

The priest asked a pretty young nun if he could kiss her goodnight after walking her back to her convent. She replied,
"Okay. But, just don't get into the habit".

A woman minister we know was fond of knitting while driving her car. One day a cop drove up next to her and yelled for her to "pull over!"
She hollered back, "Nope, it's just a scarf."

Silkworms

The new monk arrived at the monastery with only his suitcase and his pet parrot. He was greeted by the Abbot but was told that he would not be able to keep his parrot. There was a no-pet policy at the monastery.

The saddened novice asked if an exception might be made this time. The Abbot categorically refused saying that they had once made an exception and would never do so again.

The monk questioned what had gone wrong with the first exception.

The Abbot sighed and explained how they had once made an exception for two tiny silkworms, thinking they were so small and quiet, that they would fit into the cloistered environment.

The tiny silkworms were indeed popular and much beloved. The other monks would even have silent races between the two worms after Mass on Sundays.
They were evenly matched and took turns winning. Even though the worms were very popular, the racing stopped when they wound up ... in a tie.

Thrones

A Buddhist master in Malaysia died and his followers decided to store his meditation throne in a thatched building where everyone met for daily prayer. It would reside there empty, but his followers would know and be reminded that the deceased master was still there in spirit.

The monsoon rains were very strong that year and many of the thatched houses blew away. The prayer building remained, but the thatched floor was severely dampened.

One day a monk sought shelter from the rain beneath the prayer room and the floor above him gave away. The deceased master's meditation throne crashed through the damaged flooring and crushed the poor monk to death.

It was said thereafter that, 'People who live in grass houses shouldn't stow thrones'.

Symbols

Three Holy men died on Christmas day and went to Heaven. Saint Peter was waiting for them but, before he would let them in the gates, he asked each to produce something symbolizing Christmas.

The first holy man reached into his pocket and pulled out a cigarette lighter. He flicked it on and said,

"This symbolizes the Light of Christmas Spirit."

The second holy man took a set of car keys out of his pocket and shook them to produce a tingling sound saying,

"These represent the sound of Christmas Bells."

Both men were ushered into Heaven as the third and youngest of the holy man shuffled through his own pockets. Saint Peter waited patiently as the man discarded one item after another. Finally, the man held up a flimsy piece of fabric that looked like a pair of women's panties. Saint Peter frowned and asked,

"And how do these.... symbolize Christmas?"

The man in explanation just slowly hummed a bar from 'Jingle Bells' explaining that,

"These are 'Carol's'.

All three men celebrated that evening in Heaven.

Clones

Scientists at the Vatican recently made an amazing announcement. They had succeeded in the first human cloning experiment. Taking cell tissue from the Pope's fingernail, they had placed it in an embryonic cell and raised it to maturity.

Following the announcement to the astonished crowd of reporters, the Pope himself appeared on the stage podium to introduce his own clone. What appeared to be an exact twin of the Pope then appeared from behind the stage curtain.

Smiling genially, the clone raised his hand and waved to the crowd just like the real Pope. But, as the clone stepped up to the raised platform of the podium to join the Pope, his knee hit the side of the podium.

The clone grasped his knee and cursed loudly. The Pope tried to shut off the microphone but the clone blocked his way while horrifying the audience with a string of profanities.

Finally, the Pope shoved the shouting clone off the podium and apologized to the crowd. The police were called but, instead of taking away the clone, they arrested the Pope. The Pope thought it was a case of mistaken identity until he read the charges:

'Making an obscene clone fall'.

Praying Dog

A very pious Evangelical preacher had raised a small puppy from birth. Each night the preacher would say his prayers with the puppy and soon the dog learned to bow and appear to pray on it's own.

The dog was soon joining the preacher at revival meetings and the two became inseparable companions. One night, at a friend's home, the friend's German shepherd was brought out to play with the minister's dog. The minister's friend complimented the minister on his dog's pious nature, but said that his dog was also very talented.

The friend then proceeded to speak several commands to his dog. "Fetch, stand, spin, roll over, bring me my drink etc." The shepherd responded to each command instantaneously and performed each task without error. The preacher whistled in admiration and praised his friend's dog.

The friend was now proudly beaming as he inquired, "Thank you Reverend, and does your dog have any talents beside praying?"

The preacher had to stop and think for a second. He hadn't tried to teach the dog any tricks, but maybe he had learned some on his own. He decided to try one and patted his own dog's head and said gently.
"Heel."

The room sat in astonishment as the dog promptly leaped into the friend's lap, raised one paw to the friend's forehead, closed it's eyes to Heaven and woofed a blessing ...

Nero

The Roman Emperor Nero preferred to throw the early Christians to the wild beasts in his coliseum instead of crucifying them. He thought it would be less costly as well, as he would save the costs of using trained gladiators to appease the crowd's thirst for blood.

But, the Emperor's chief accountant explained that they were actually losing money by doing so.

"How could that be," asked Nero?

The answer, "The lions were eating up all the prophets."

Diets

Father O'lardo was the heaviest priest the bishop had ever seen. His appetite was prodigious and it was not uncommon at a meal for O'lardo to eat several chickens, a loaf of bread covered in butter, a pot of mashed potatoes and several ears of corn before asking for extra helpings of dessert and then washing it all down with a bottle of wine.

The bishop decided it was time to visit the hefty priest and found him reclined back in his favorite chair. O'Lardo's stomach protruded massively from his robes and the bishop ordered that,

"Father O'lardo, your stomach has gotten too big. It is time for you to diet."

To which O'lardo replied,

"Okay bishop... What color?"

Painting the Church

The largest Presbyterian Church in St. Louis, Mo. decided to hire a Scottish painting company to repaint the entire exterior of the church. The owner of the painting company, Mr. Angus McGroin, was officially a member of the congregation but it had been many years since he had been seen at any services.

McGroin was a skilled painter but was known to be a bit tight when it came time to pay his bills or donate to the church. That aside, McGroin arrived bright and early to begin the job and started putting up ladders, scaffolding and lifts.

When it came time to buy the white paint, McGroin tried to order the exact amount. But when he got back to the site, he realized it wouldn't be enough. Instead of going back to the store for more paint, McGroin waited until no one was looking and added a couple of gallons of paint thinner to each can to stretch the coverage.

McGroin spent the rest of the day painting and was almost finished when the sky darkened and a heavy rain began falling. He watched helplessly as the thunder rumbled and the fresh new paint began to drip.

The drips became puddles, the puddles merged into streams and soon the entire lawn and driveway of the church were covered in the telltale white blotches.

McGroin knew inside that this was a judgment from God to punish his act of skullduggery. Bemoaning his fate, McGroin threw himself to the ground with fists raised to heaven and prayed for forgiveness crying,

"Oh God, I am truly sorry. What can I do to make it up to you."

The thunder quelled and a powerful voice from above spoke,

"REPAINT AND THIN NO MORE."

State Fair

A Mormon boy was away from Utah on his first mission to a small town in upstate New York. There he met two pretty Jewish sisters named Beth and Louise who lived next door. The young man screwed up his courage one day and asked Louise to go to the State Fair with him.

Louise agreed and when they arrived, the Mormon asked his date what she would like to do first? She replied, "Get weighed'

There just happened to be a carnival barker next to them at a weighing booth. Our Mormon boy helped Louise up onto the weighing scale and the barker predicted she would weigh 120 lbs.. The scale, when released read 109 lbs and the barker handed Louise a large stuffed bear as a prize for his inaccuracy.

They went on the Ferris wheel with the bear in-arm but Louise seemed to not be enjoying it. When the wheel stopped, the boy asked her what she'd like to do next. She replied, "Get weighed".

The Mormon boy shook his head but found another weighing booth where Louise's weight was again estimated and when weighed, she won another teddy bear.

They then each had some fast food and a drink and the boy asked again what else she would like to do. He cringed a bit as she replied once more, "Get weighed."

They were soon in possession of a third huge stuffed bear and the young man was getting tired of carrying them around. He took Louise home and dropped her and the bears off before leaving quickly & thinking how strange these 'New Yorkers' were.

Louise's sister Beth met her at the door as the Mormon boy disappeared down the street. Noticing how crestfallen her sister looked, she asked how the evening had gone. Louise looked sadly up and replied.
"Wousy."

Leftovers

A 'flasher' appeared recently in a confessional. When asked if he felt truly contrite and ready to sin no more, he replied only, that he had decided to,
'Stick it out for just one more year."

The new church minister was rumored to have a strange sense of humor. This proved to indeed be the case when he decided to relocate the church cemetery next to the county hospice. This in itself wasn't so strange, until you read the new sign he had placed out in front of the newly dug graves...
'Home for the Terminally Still'.

The same minister decided to raise some revenue for the church by selling 'blessed' coffins to the members of his congregation for their family members. Again, this wasn't so strange, until he started adding, 'lifetime warrantees'.

Air conditioning was recently added to the monastery's dormitory but not to the adjacent barn. That summer an animal rights group complained that the poor horses were suffering from the heat. The bishop was called in to explain that air conditioning was only for 'humid beings'.

Brother Jimmy was a bit of a problem at the monastery. In civilian life he had worked at a muffler shop but he left it to join the Franciscans because he found it was too 'exhausting'.
The other brothers tried to find a spot for him in the kitchen deli but he 'couldn't cut the mustard'. When asked to add spices to the soup, he said he 'didn't have enough thyme' to do it

right. He also didn't like making the morning coffee saying, it was always 'the same old grind'.

He was finally asked to leave the kitchen when his orange juice came out too watery because he 'couldn't concentrate'.

Putting him in charge of the monastery's pool didn't work either because he found it too 'draining'.

The bishop decided to let him lead the monks in their morning exercises but he wasn't 'fit' for the job. As a last resort, Jimmy was given the monks' old robes to mend any holes he found. Jimmy quit at the end of the day because he thought it was only a 'sew-sew job' and he wasn't really 'suited' for it.

The last we heard, Brother Jimmy had gone back to school to become a doctor but that at his new office, he didn't have enough 'patience'.

The bishop had a real interest in modern science. He was reading a book about anti-gravity and wound up without any sleep. He said he just 'couldn't put it down'.

A friend of ours opened a dry-cleaning business right next to the Catholic Church convent. He got off on the wrong foot when he knocked at the front door and asked the Mother Superior if she had any dirty habits.

When I finished typing these puns, my fingers were very painful. I went to the doctor but he told me not to worry because it was only a minor case of 'Authoritis'.

Conclusion

SAUL of TARSUS

Knock Knock

Who's There?

Saul.

Saul who?

Saul there is, there ain't no more.

That's 'Sol' Folks!

Additional copies of this book can be obtained by ordering through Amazon.com, Borders.com, Bowker's Books in Print, BookData UK, PubStock, or directly from Trafford Publishing at Trafford.com bookstore. Toll free 1-888-232-4444.
For more information, visit us at our web page under Angels Laughing at www.Trafford.com/05-0690.

Printed in the United Kingdom
by Lightning Source UK Ltd.
116696UKS00001B/26